BALANCING THREE

BALANCING THREE

Carol Debra Lefkowitz Jones

ACME PUBLISHING

2017

ACME PUBLISHING

Balancing Three
Copyright 2017 by Carol Debra Lefkowitz Jones
All rights reserved. www.balancingthree.com

No part of this book may be used or reproduced in any form, stored in any retrieval system, or transmitted in any manner by any means—electronic, mechanical, photocopy, recording, or otherwise—without prior written permission of the publisher, except as provided by United States of America copyright law.

This book contains nonfiction stories. Some names and identifying details have been changed to protect the privacy of individuals.

FIRST EDITION

ISBN: 978-0-9995810-0-1 (paperback)
       978-0-9995810-1-8 (hardcover)

For information about ordering additional copies or copyright permissions, please contact:
ACME Publishing at (626) 227-1188 extension 108.

For press and speaking engagements, please contact:
Carol Jones at (626) 227-1188 extension 101.

Balancing Three—Jones, Carol Debra Lefkowitz.
1. Parenting. 2. Motherhood. 3. Raising Triplets. 4. Memoir.
5. Fertility. 6. Pregnancy

Printed in the U.S.A.

*This book is dedicated to my parents.
I love you, Mom and Dad!*

Contents

Preface 9
A Bit of Background 12
Battling the Urge for Perfection 25
Why Motherhood? 32
Enter Stage Right...Triplets! 37
Getting Ready for Babies 47
Nursing (or Not!) 52
Taking the Triplets to Hollywood 55
How Do You Do It? 65
Are They Identical? 68
Happy Preparations 73
Bottles and Toilet Training 79
Finding the Perfect Nanny 84
Mommy and Me Activities 90
Parenting Classes 90
One Room or Three? 93
Getting Ready for Pre-school 97
The Tooth Fairy 102
Daddy 105
It's Time for Momma to Take a Break ... 109
Managing Time 113
Out of Control 119
Are We Having Fun Yet? 126
Beware of Hand-Me-Downs 131

Less is More	134
Shopping	140
Managing Three	146
Sleepovers	152
A Few House Rules	155
Too Much TV	159
Less is More Part II	161
A Mother's Love	169
It's that Time of Year Again	173
Birthdays and the Holidays	177
Monday Mornings	181
Lily's Wants	187
Are they Identical? Part II	190
The Balance between Three and Me	197
Choices	202
Parting Thoughts	207
Answers to Commonly	209
Asked Questions	209
Resources	214
Acknowledgements	216

Preface

Who the Heck Am I Writing This For Anyway?

When I think about my reasons for writing, I realize that there are many.

First and foremost, I hope that anyone who takes the time to read this account of my experiences as a triplet mom will find the stories useful in some way. Second, but no less important, I hope that you will find these accounts entertaining. Because let's face it, we all can use at least an occasional break from the pressures of life.

While writing about my life as a triplet mom, I was able to take my own break, and breathe, really breathe. I don't always seem to manage that during the course of my day.

Balancing Three is a collection of my experiences as a triplet mom, including a handful of tips and tricks for dealing with "trips," as we sometimes call it. Maybe you'll relate as you read about my struggles and successes with life's basic challenges as a parent, including the most important and perhaps most tenuous, the effort to take care of myself while taking care of my family. I've become my own coach, and my own cheerleader. With a few added and frequent prayers up to the powers that be.

I have to remind myself to be forgiving, of course to others, but more importantly to myself, in the face of sometimes daily self-reproach. And I'm guessing I'm not alone in doubting myself repeatedly. Probably not many of us parents are that kind to ourselves. So if you tend to put yourself last on your own to-do list, I hope that putting yourself first (at least some of the time) will become a new habit for you.

I hope to make you laugh, or even cry, and by this book's end to put your own experiences in perspective as you read the account of this triplet mom who juggles, multi-tasks, and manages to fit in "just one more thing" to allow her life to run more smoothly, more comfortably, and most happily.

Thanks for letting me share a little of your day.

I hope that when you finish this book you'll be smiling,

stepping a little lighter, and holding a greater appreciation for yourself.

With warm wishes,

Carol

A Bit of Background

At the time of this writing, my triplet daughters are eight years old. Time flies, and it no longer seems like yesterday that my girls were in diapers. The triplet stroller is long gone. It hits me somewhere near my heart that even our playground days won't last forever. Before long the girls will finish elementary school, and then junior high. Even high school graduation is only ten years away and then the girls will be off to college (we hope).

My eyes tear up as I reminisce about all the stages we've already passed through together: breastfeeding (all three weeks of it), cribs, crawling, walking, talking, bottle feeding, diapers, and even appearing on TV. Each phase has had its own set of challenges and abundance of precious and memorable moments.

When I think about the days when I can give myself my very own "Superstar" sticker, I realize that those are the times that I am most relaxed, least stressed, and least overwhelmed. These happen also to be the times that I'm ready, willing, and able really to *be* with my kids. And it's already happening that they don't always want or need me, so in the sense that I've instilled in my girls a spirit of independence and self-sufficiency, perhaps I've done at least that one thing right. I don't mean to diminish the extent of my impact and I'm sure I've done more than one thing right. Maybe being self-deprecating is a bad habit that I should get over.

It's funny, but every time I sit down to write about what I do to raise my kids, I keep circling back to what I'm doing to take care of my own needs. As the years go by, I've found that making myself a priority has become mandatory to my ability to manage my load. Let's just say that self-care has become quite high on my list of tricks. When I'm happy, I'm happy with them. When I'm distraught, harried, hassled, and angry, that's also what they see. I don't think it's the "me" that they prefer, either. So it's not a stretch at all to conclude that the "happy" me is my better self when it comes to mothering—or anything else for that matter. So I've made it my goal to make myself as happy as possible. That's wonderfully ironic, I think. Not to mention, a win-win-win-win.

I grew up on Long Island, New York, and spent my childhood summers in the Catskills, back when the Catskills were teeming with families from Queens, Brooklyn and the Bronx looking to get away from the summer heat. My parents owned what's called a bungalow colony there, which is essentially a bunch of cottages surrounding a sprawling lawn, with a common pool and a couple of swing sets scattered about. The moms and kids of these vacationing families moved in for the summer, the kids attending the day camp there. The dads, for the most part, came up only on weekends, continuing to work Monday through Friday throughout the summer.

Like all the other kids, I attended the day camp when I was little. I remember standing around the thirty-foot flagpole with all the other campers at the end of each camp day. The camp director would ceremoniously lower the flag down the pole each afternoon while we sang "Taps."

I remember feeling a bubble of anticipation for the song

to end, because when it was over, we shouted in unison "Supper!" and scattered, running in various directions to our respective bungalows to see what was being served up by our moms on our outdoor picnic tables.

Summers were the highlight of my childhood. The school years themselves were fraught with parental and social pressures, and weren't nearly as much fun as those much-anticipated summer months.

My dad was trained in the military, and later became a trial lawyer. He parented his three kids with the apparent expectation of us all achieving perfection—at least by his own measure of that seemingly elusive goal. Flattered and encouraged by my proud parents, I took the offered opportunity to skip third grade, generally got straight A's, and graduated high school just shy of my seventeenth birthday. Looking back, I see now that I was quite a young pup to be considering my options in the world at that early time in my life.

Following a philosophical discussion with my parents regarding practical versus impractical college pursuits, I set aside the information on music schools that I had been researching, and went to Johns Hopkins University, in

Baltimore, Maryland, to study something other than music or medicine. I really wasn't quite sure what my college focus would be, and I admit to feeling a bit lost in contemplating my options. It was true I didn't envision myself as a performance star, despite my love of singing and playing the piano and guitar. And I didn't know enough then to even begin to consider any of the ancillary music-related career options I might have considered, had I gone the creative route. So I listened to my parents as their dutiful daughter, and moved on to consider the other more traditional future career options available to me.

I started my college career with a major in International Relations. Within very short order I realized that International Relations had little to do with the foreign languages I loved (French, Spanish, and Hebrew). Alas, International Relations, I quickly learned, had much more to do with Political Science, for which I had little to no interest, and politics in general, for which I had already developed a marked distaste.

I quickly changed my major to Economics, which didn't really suggest a clear career choice upon graduation, and didn't exactly thrill my heart, but there I was. I graduated with a B.A. from Hopkins, a 3.8 grade point average, and little idea of how I would spend the rest of my life.

I considered two promising job offers afforded by my high grades and highly-regarded school degree. One was a job with a money management firm in Manhattan, and another was as an assistant and research analyst to an economist at the Federal Reserve Board in Washington, D.C., I chose the latter, primarily due to my preference for green pastures rather than the concrete pavement of the Big Apple. Not necessarily the best reasoning, but once again, I was still young, twenty-one at the time.

After two short years at the "Fed," as it's commonly known, I found that I had cultivated an intolerance for computer programs and programming. What now? I remembered the ten days I had spent touring the coast of California before entering college. I thought about my continued interest in music, my indulgence in what had become my hobby having included college level courses in improvisation and music composition, with the occasional coffeehouse performance, just me and my guitar. With no real career plan, I decided to go west and settle in Los Angeles, California. I was twenty-three.

18   Balancing Three

I pondered my next move. What's an outgoing young Jewish New Yorker with a college degree in Economics to do ... in Southern California? After an afternoon admiring the view of the Pacific Ocean from the main commercial street in Manhattan Beach, I took the California real estate sales exam, thinking that this might be the perfect field for me. I ultimately opted for a position with a commercial real estate brokerage firm (better hours than residential brokerage) and I eventually landed in the unlikely specialization of industrial real estate brokerage. As a broker/salesperson, I walked door to door, or more precisely, warehouse to warehouse, looking for leads to turn into leases and sales in the competitive Los Angeles brokerage marketplace. I was also one of a handful of females in this sub-specialty, and at times found myself in the middle of a conversation that felt like it should be taking place in a men's locker room, and not a professional office. I took it in stride, and learned to blend in, as much as I could anyway, with the last name "Lefkowitz."

I struggled my way through the early 1990s just barely making a living. By the time I finally was making some money, I was sick of the business. After ten years, I had hit my limit. It was time to move on. I left brokerage to join a small family-owned construction and real estate development firm, and learned the ins and outs of industrial building design and development, and a few necessary facts about construction. I was still in sales, like brokerage, but now I was selling construction and custom-built buildings. My creativity also finally had an outlet, as my role included facilitating the preliminary site-planning design of our customers' building projects.

But a love relationship eluded me. In the scheme of my life, I was burning through my 30s. Don't get me wrong, I enjoyed some aspects of being single. But underneath my appearance as a "fun-loving girl," I was waiting for a permanent love relationship to appear. Right or wrong, I felt like certain things would have to be "on hold," so to speak, until I finally became part of a twosome. I remember my dad asking me what my five-year plan was. Truth was, I didn't have one. I held off on purchasing a home, thinking that this was a step for a married person. Call me a traditionalist.

Turning forty caused me to take stock of my life. I realized that if I wanted a family, I needed to attend seriously to the business of looking for a mate, and to stop being a playgirl, lusting after younger men, who weren't ready financially or really mature enough yet, for marriage. That had been fun for a while, for sure, but I wasn't especially interested in being a sugar momma. And often my sexual targets were young enough to be unsettled—professionally, emotionally—you name it. I eventually drew the conclusion that if I wanted an equal partner or, better yet, a partner that I could look up to and learn from, I needed to look in the "older men" category.

Once I set the intention of finding my mate, I did it in earnest. I made a "Top Ten" list of all my "must-haves" for my perfect partner:

1. 5'9" or taller (to top my height of nearly 5'6", and leave room for heels ;))
2. Good sense of humor
3. Intelligent
4. Successful
5. Likes to dance
6. Good body/good chemistry with me
7. Attractive
8. Masculine (no wimpy momma's boys for me!)
9. Outgoing

10. Could be ten years older than me

I came across one of my earlier versions of this list when cleaning out my garage recently. My original list had 12 requisites, then 11, as I eliminated what I perceived as an obstacle to finding my perfect mate. It seems there's help from the universe when you actually write things down. From my experience, it works.

I stopped waiting for the rest of my life to happen "someday." I bought a piece of real estate instead of waiting to get married first. I leased a BMW, just for fun. I stopped dating younger men (or even age-appropriate men) who didn't have two nickels to rub together. My search for my life partner was "on."

Things unfolded like magic after that.

In September 2004, my future husband, Simon, showed up as a new employee at the small firm where I'd been working for six years. It was love at first sight. Simon had salt and pepper hair (which has since turned to nearly all salt), was eleven years my senior, and built like a rock. He had a great smile, was funny, and fun to be with. I didn't get bored at all during our conversations, which had been a problem with other potential mate candidates. And most importantly, Simon met my 5'9" or taller height requirement. Check, check, check!

He seemed to be the perfect, relaxed complement to what had become my personality—yes, I'll say it—an "A" type. On that point appearances can be deceiving. Simon has since proven that for him relaxation doesn't easily go hand-in-hand with running a business and parenting triplet girls.

Simon had been married before, and had already raised two grown sons who were in their 20s. He'd been divorced for ten years, seemingly a long enough period for him to be ready to commit to a new relationship.

Simon confidently (and with humor) addressed my "40 Questions" on each of our early dates. I needed to sniff out whether or not there was potential to our work flirtation turning into a serious and long-term relationship. OK, so maybe it wasn't 40 questions. But it was a lot. I wasn't interested in a fling, of that I was sure. So I teed up my questions and waited to see if he passed my test. My main two questions were centered around marriage and children.

"Are you interested in getting married again?"

"Yes," he responded.

"Do you want more kids?"

"Yes" again, was his enthusiastic answer.

All of Simon's answers were what I wanted to hear. There were no big red flags. Everything pointed toward the possibility of a rosy future. I eventually ran out of things to ask him.

"What? No more questions?" Simon inquired with a smile, sometime during our tenth or so date. I hadn't peppered him with this or that long-range goals-related question during the appetizer course of our meal.

"I'm all out," I admitted. "Now we just need to see if we get along."

We were happy, we were in love, and we let the bosses know we were serious after keeping things a secret for the first two months. In my mind, to put it in real estate terms, this was a done deal. And finally, after a two-year courtship (which felt LOOOONG...story for another day), we tied the knot.

Simon and I decided, not long after, to form our own construction company. We were actively trying to get pregnant, and this seemed like the perfect long-term plan. Theory was, if we were both self-employed, I would have some flexibility with my schedule once I became a mom. So, a year after getting married, Simon and I became business partners as well, and we formed our own building and engineering construction firm.

So that's a little, or maybe a lot, about me. Working wife, business owner, finally settled down after years of being single. What's in store for me next? Triplets, apparently!

Battling the Urge for Perfection

Everyone asks me, "How do you do it?" Raising triplets, that is. Acquaintances, strangers, and even cashiers in the grocery store, all want to know if I have a special secret. At least once or twice a month, I hear some remark or another.

"Triplets?! What's that like??" or "Triplets?! G-d bless you."

"You're my hero," one mom of twins recently exclaimed, acknowledging my heavier load.

I've had more than one person tell me that I should write a book, detailing my experiences of exactly what it's like, in fact, to have and raise triplets. I heard the suggestion enough times that I finally decided to take on the challenge.

It's not easy, it's true. But then again, I really don't know any different. Lately I've taken to jigsaw puzzles to preserve my sanity. Somehow, when sitting quietly, looking for the perfect puzzle piece, my concerns and worries float away. Like Simon and his morning Sudoku ritual, for me doing jigsaw puzzles allows the concerns of my life to dissipate, at least momentarily. Writing works too. Now the trick is making time to *do* jigsaw puzzles, or to write. Good luck to me.

The short answer is, I don't know *how* I do it, I just do it. I should mention my nearly daily consumption of good chardonnay (or pinot noir) in the evening, just to slow me down. Because the reality is...I don't stop. From the moment I wake up until the girls are in bed at night, and even after, I'm on the go.

Now I've done my share of personal development seminars over the years. One particularly illuminating class explained that there's a correlation between one's childhood experiences and one's adult mindset. This gave me new insight into my own behavior, and I realized that my perfectionist tendencies have been driving me.

My trial lawyer dad somehow couldn't seem to leave the courtroom behind. At the dinner table growing up, we learned not to speak unless we were absolutely certain that what we had to say was the truth, the whole truth and nothing but the truth, so help us G-d. If I wasn't 100% sure of the accuracy of what I had to share, let's say I was 90% sure, I knew better than to open my mouth. And school tests? If I got a 98%, the response was generally: "What happened to the other two percent?" So I learned to try to be perfect.

One area that I had difficulty mastering as a child, and still do, was keeping my room neat. I threw everything into my bedroom closet every time my dad asked me to clean my room. The sliding closet door would barely close, it was so packed with G-d knows what. I remember one time Dad was looking for something and thought it was in my bedroom closet. He slid the closet door open, and everything that had been jammed in there came cascading down onto the floor of my bedroom.

As a punishment for my indisputably imperfect tidying-up skills, I was sent out of the house that afternoon, with instructions to find somewhere else to sleep that night. I think I might've been eleven or twelve years old at the time. I walked the block-and-a-half to my best friend Teresa's house, majorette baton in hand for "protection." Mom stood by worriedly, after making sure I had said baton in hand, knowing she would be ineffective in protesting my dad's chosen punishment. This was the early 1970s, and it just was accepted by both of us that his decision was final.

Teresa's Chinese immigrant parents found it more than odd, I'm sure, but they never turned me away, and on the more than one occasion that I found myself on their doorstep, requesting entry for the night, they welcomed me in with puzzled expressions. Now even by yesterday's standards, this may have been viewed as more than harsh, as parenting techniques go, but this story is not about that. And whatever lesson I was supposed to learn by that punishment didn't quite work, because up until recently my house was quite a mess. I saw the mess, but to me it was normal, and to be expected. Because what the hell, I have triplets. How the heck is one supposed to have an immaculate house with (then toddler) triplets?

In any event, this life lesson was, and is, apparently one that I'm supposed to learn. Similar to the rage my father exhibited upon opening my bedroom closet door, it eventually became clear that my husband was going out of his mind with the disorder.

He asked me one day, "Do I need to sleep somewhere

else?"

It wasn't intended as a joke, and it wasn't a threat either. At least I didn't take it that way. It was just his way of telling me that the various stacks of miscellaneous mail, or other paperwork, or small toys or other tiny items in counter corners, etc., weren't okay with him. And that marked the beginning of my attempt to bring my perfectionist tendencies to the area of our household organization. Housekeeper or no, the papers needed a place to go.

If you're curious, I wouldn't necessarily characterize my husband as a perfectionist. But he is most certainly at his best on the rare occasions when the house is immaculate. That condition generally occurs on the days we have company over. Sadly, household organization is a skill that I haven't mastered just yet.

So now, fortunately (or unfortunately), I'm able to see the house through his eyes. And I sit down, and look to the right and think to myself, "there's dust on the floor," and up I go to get a broom and dust pan.

I sit back down and then glance at our kitchen table thinking, "Uh-oh. What are those papers doing there?" and I'm on my feet again. You get the idea.

But since all work and no play makes Momma a bit cranky, I recently set the modest goal of enjoying at least a few moments of fun with my kids each day. It doesn't need to be much to make my day complete. Some days it's a tickle fight, other days it's watching them do their newest "routine" on our backyard trampoline. Just a little each day, that's all I need. And if only a few moments sounds like too little, you could be right, but the day goes by fast. I try to give our girls the attention that they need too, and not let my OCD regarding keeping the house tidy unneccessarily skew my priorities.

I set a second, albeit possibly more challenging, goal of making it through the day without yelling (more on anger management later). I don't condone yelling as a parenting technique, but lately, with the girls' focus on their iPhones, computers, or the TV, it's one way to break through the trance.

I've managed my first goal reasonably well. Jury's out on my second goal performance, which is definitely short of perfect—oh well. Writing gives me peace, so lately I'm doing that as much as I can.

Here's my advice, you can take it or leave it: When you're

juggling kids, a spouse, and a business, find your source of joy and then make it a priority.

Remember the flight attendant's instructions to parents to give themselves oxygen first, and then to their children? Somehow in my day to day, I can easily forget to implement that most excellent suggestion. Some days I forget to eat, after serving breakfast to everyone else. And I often don't get enough sleep, after arranging the evening so that my daughters are in bed and asleep by 8 p.m. It's *so* hard to shut the mind off after it's been spinning all day. And on and on. Lately, I've found that the use of prayer, when it comes to acceptance, peace of mind, business goals, or anything else for that matter, is as effective as any technique I've known. Power of the universe, and G-d above—thank heavens for it.

Ready or not, life marches on.

Why Motherhood?

I'm guilty of wanting some form of immortality, I suppose—a piece of myself that continues into the future. Or some evidence that my life on earth has had some meaning. And that desire, to leave something of myself behind, is also a motivation for writing. One day, even after I'm gone, someone can read these words and maybe find them relatable. And in this way, my life will have some added posterity. I was here; I passed through. Here's my footprint, so to speak, a small memento of my existence on this earth. And who knows? Maybe my sharing will make a positive difference in someone else's life.

My mom graduated Phi Beta Kappa from New York University. After marrying my dad in the 1950s, she essentially became a "stay-at-home" mom. In fact, she worked consistently, but it just didn't appear that way to me, because she worked with my dad in his home office. So from my vantage point, she was always around, more or less available, and dedicated to helping (and loving) her children.

I somehow thought my mom wasn't fulfilled by her work with my dad. I never actually asked her if she was or if she wasn't. I just sort of assumed she wasn't, as it didn't appear to be fulfilling a life career goal of her own. Not unusual during her generation, I might add.

I suppose it was a criticism I was making in a way, thinking that supporting my dad's career and having time for her children wasn't a worthy enough objective. But hey, I was young when I graduated high school and college. You think you know everything when you're nineteen, don't you?

In any event, as mentioned, I delayed getting married. It was partly because I didn't find the right match early on, but also because I made my financial success a primary objective. *I* was going to support myself, and *I* was going to have a career. I figured marriage and kids could wait until after I had had a life "of my own." Those goals were always there, lurking in the background, as in "one day...", but they were something that would happen in the vague future. In my mind, having a career, doing something that was all about me, was first. That mattered. And then it took me over. It nearly defined me.

I worked long hours for years, with little income to show for it. Eventually, right about the time I was losing my enthusiasm for this career thing, I began to see some results from my labors, and I started to make money more easily. But contrary to my expectations, I didn't find the whole venture at all fulfilling. It was a career, that's true, something to do and by which to make a living, but I was ready to focus on someone else for a change. That's when the switch flipped. Suddenly the thing that was a priority was finding a mate.

I also began taking an interest in spirituality. What's the meaning of my life, I wondered? It wasn't explained, as I recalled, during services at the Jewish temple we attended when I was preparing for my Bat-mitzvah (Jewish coming of age ceremony).

While I always had planned to have children, suddenly this subject took on a new relevance. Why am I here, anyway? Maybe having children would somehow justify my existence, and, from a vanity perspective I suppose, carry on the impact of my having lived here on this earth.

In hindsight, the eighteen years I spent in real estate before getting married is a bit of a blur. Somehow, the money I finally made after years of hard work, while it created an ease and flow to things, wasn't a substitute for a permanent relationship. Something was still missing. And sowing my wild oats, while it certainly was fun—well, the buzz wasn't lasting that long. I had reached the point where my "it's all about me" attitude just wasn't particularly satisfying any more.

So here I am, twenty-five plus years later, and finally I'm a mom. I do feel complete now in many ways. Is that being selfish? I hope not. I love my daughters, and they love me. Being loved is a good thing. As a mom, you give and you give and you give…and then you get an enormous love in return.

I try to do my best as a parent. I give my girls hugs and kisses every day. Lately we've been having tickle fights, which elicits bubbles of giggles from them and broad smiles from me and my husband. I serve healthy food, and limit the girls' sugar consumption. I try to teach (and exhibit) good manners. And the girls all speak French as a result of the dual language elementary school they attend, a choice that we hope will lead to unusual and wonderful adventures when they become adults. My mothering choices and decisions face me daily, as they likely will for the rest of my life.

Parenting—it's a journey—and a challenge.

And for the record—I'm in it to win it.

(My very own Superstar sticker, that is.)

Enter Stage Right...Triplets!

"When did you know you were having triplets?" I've been asked.

"Right away," I answer.

Like many responsible unmarried couples, we used precautions and waited until after we were married before trying to get pregnant. As you might imagine, the odds were stacked against natural conception at the age of forty-three. Simon was fifty-four, which annoyingly didn't interfere with his childbearing capabilities. After much research I found a fertility doctor Simon and I both liked and trusted, and we embarked upon the scary but exciting fertility journey toward parenthood.

"Did you know it was three girls?!" is often the follow up question from my awestruck new acquaintance.

"The geneticist had to double check," I reply, "since triplets of the same gender are so uncommon." True statement. So yes, I knew I was having triplets almost right away, and learned after only about ten short weeks later that I was expecting three baby girls.

I had suffered a miscarriage during my first pregnancy, which we later learned was due to that first embryo having insufficient chromosomes to survive. My husband and I had felt that loss deeply, but we were committed to becoming parents together. Once we got our doctor's approval, we rallied ourselves for another go at becoming pregnant.

This next part is graphic, okay? During our fertility treatment, my husband and I created embryos, which were frozen and stored in what the doctor referred to as "straws." I vaguely recall seeing the straws which weren't too unlike drinking straws, if I remember correctly. Ours were filled with five embryos each. For my first insemination (and resulting pregnancy), we had put in two fresh embryos.

Sadly, when you thaw the frozen straws to prepare for insemination, only some of the embryos survive.

"When you are using frozen embryos, your odds of pregnancy decrease," our doctor said. "So you can put in three embryos to increase your odds," she added. "Up to three embryos is considered statistically safe."

"What are the odds of triplets?" we naturally asked. Obvious question, right?

"Very, very low odds," was the answer. Less than a hundredth of a percent, apparently, not even worth contemplating.

After my three embryos were inseminated, I went on the standard protocol forty-eight hours bed rest, which was followed by taking a blood test to see if the venture had been successful. Would I be pregnant? The blood test would tell.

The numbers were off the chart. My hCG level, (this stands for Human Chorionic Gonadotropin hormone; don't worry, there's not going to be a test on this) the hormone used to detect pregnancy, was more than double that of my first pregnancy. I knew right away that a triple pregnancy was likely.

So what did I feel? Elated? Thrilled? Happy beyond belief?

What I felt, more precisely, was gripped with fear and worry. Worry that I would miscarry. Deep fear that the children would not be born healthy. Plain, immeasurable,

40 Balancing Three

overwhelming worry.

I need to share that I'm a deep believer in the Law of Attraction, the ability to manifest what is in our minds and to turn those thoughts into reality. In fact, I attribute my triplet pregnancy to a little playful story I scribed during my forty-eight hours bed rest immediately following my embryo insemination. I had read about scribing (which is just a synonym for writing) from a book written by Esther and Jerry Hicks called, "Ask and It Is Given." The book suggests scribing about your intended or hoped for outcome with a sense of playfulness.

So, I wrote about my little embryos finding a spot to sleep somewhere on the wall of my womb. In my first version of this story, two of my embryos were squabbling over the same spot. Could happen, right? But then I realized, thankfully, that two embryos fighting over the same spot would likely mean that neither would lodge there successfully. So I crossed out the line I had just written and wrote instead that each embryo had found its own perfect spot on the lining of my womb. They wished each other goodnight, "Goodnight A! Goodnight B! Goodnight C!" as they were then named, in the style of the old TV show, *The Waltons*, if you're old enough to remember that show. I smiled to myself and put the story down.

A week later, if memory serves me right, I got the news... it was a triplet pregnancy!

Miracle, you ask? Yes. Definitely. Attributable to the power of positive thought and the law of attraction—in addition to science? Quite possibly.

So I embarked upon my 37½ week journey toward motherhood, a mother already, entrusted by G-d with the job of carrying these newly forming beings safely into our world.

As I had already witnessed the possible power of my writing, with my triplet pregnancy outcome, I worried that negative or fearful thinking could equally create undesirable outcomes. So I tasked myself with attempting to rid my brain of any negative or worrisome thoughts.

Good luck! It was next to impossible. Having been through one miscarriage before the happy news of this new pregnancy, I was grimly aware that time needed to pass before the pregnancy was secure. I fretted, I worried, I read and I researched. And the more I researched the outcomes of triplet pregnancies, the less secure I felt.

To make matters worse, my fertility doctor proposed we consult with a specialist in something called selective reduction. Perhaps you can deduce what that means. She made the suggestion as if she were recommending a neutral consultant to provide pros and cons of such a procedure, which was not the case. This specialist knew how to terminate the life of one embryo while theoretically not disturbing the other two.

Horrible, horrible thought. The process was sickening to contemplate. The selective reduction specialist provided decades-old data suggesting her procedure created less risk than that already inherent in a triplet pregnancy. I didn't believe it. I did my own Google research, which yielded different data, suggesting equal risks for tampering with the pregnancy vs. the risks of the triplet pregnancy itself. We didn't deliberate further. We told the selective reduction specialist we would not be requiring her services, and steeled ourselves to bravely meet the perils and risks that we might encounter in the months ahead.

I had now fully educated myself as to all the statistics. Here were the facts: many multiple pregnancies fail, many end with tragic results: some with extended NICU stays for newborns (neo-natal intensive care units, if you're not familiar with the term), and some triplets are born with lifelong impairments. I felt elated and depressed all at once. I was figuratively and literally weighed down by the responsibility of safely carrying the babies to full term. My perfectionism became fully blown in my desire to do this right. I bled early in my pregnancy and was again put on bed rest, for six weeks. But G-d was determined to bless me, and the blood clot dissipated.

I prayed, I rested, and I tried in vain not to worry. I made it to twenty-six weeks, a major milestone in the objective of delivering a healthy baby, single, twin, or triplet.

At that point I went on semi-leave and tried to "work" from home for two more weeks, taking advantage of a little flux in my doctor's instructions. I wasn't yet ready to leave my familiar work routine. At twenty-eight weeks I finally surrendered to my body and went on official pregnancy leave.

I remember looking out the window of my bedroom during this last period of time before the girls were born. Our bedroom overlooked the street, and I left the curtains open so that I could see outside and contemplate how my life was about to change. It was autumn, and the tall liquid amber tree next to our driveway had beautiful leaves of all colors, some green, some yellow, some burnt orange, and some even a deep shade of red.

We live on a cul-de-sac, so only a few cars drove past the window as the hours passed, and they were mostly neighbors, with the occasional passerby looking to evaluate the neighborhood. I watched the leaves change color on that tree while I lay in bed with my hands on my growing belly. I waited. I was worried and nervously happy. I worked hard and in vain to dispel all the negative thoughts swirling through my head. I repeated positive mantras to try to clear my mind...and waited some more. I was virtually frozen in place, hands on my belly, trying to control the tempest of thoughts in my mind. I didn't read aloud. Despite my love of music, I don't even recall singing aloud. I just lay in bed, waiting for December 12th, the scheduled due date, to arrive.

I felt very little movement from my babies during my pregnancy, which increased my worry, even though my ultrasounds continued to show things were fine and that babies A, B and C were all growing steadily.

I made it to thirty weeks—and then to thirty-two. I informed my husband that our weekly date dining out was "off" until further notice, as I could no longer sit up at a table comfortably.

At thirty-seven weeks—the week my girls were due—my blood pressure shot up, and my legs got swollen from retained water. I was admitted for observation to Huntington Hospital in Pasadena, California. I had gained sixty-five pounds. The swelling and high blood pressure were signs of a condition called preeclampsia, which occurs only during pregnancy. For the next forty-eight hours I was hooked up to three monitors and awakened every four hours. When they attached the plastic monitor wires all over my belly, I couldn't move more than two inches in either direction. I waited until my scheduled C-section two days later (and 37.5 weeks into my pregnancy), getting almost no sleep at all until the morning of Friday, December 12, 2008.

Babies A, B and C were born at 8:01, 8:02 and 8:03 a.m., at 4 lbs. 14 oz., 4 lbs. 1 oz., and 4 lbs. 13 oz. respectively, a total of 13 lbs. 12 oz. of beautiful baby girls. My pregnancy had been successful, and my new job was about to begin.

I slept for the next several hours as the anesthesia wore

off, marking the transition in my life to mother of three. When I awoke, I took a deep breath, giving myself just a moment before embracing all my new fears and worries as a new mother. My delivery complete, I could proudly boast that I had birthed three healthy, beautiful little baby girls.

Getting Ready for Babies

We hired Maria two weeks before my due date. I was effectively bedridden at this point, too large to really move around easily, and the doctor had advised me to lay low. Maria brought me meals in bed and cleaned the house. She spoke only Spanish, a limitation I thought we could adjust to. Who knew? Maybe the babies would learn to speak Spanish. I dusted off my high school Spanish skills and installed myself in the position of sole family communicator with our new full-time helper.

In my last few weeks of pregnancy I also hired Rosa for what we referred to as "night nannying." This is not to be confused with the services of a night nurse, who would've cost 50% more. These two hires were perhaps my most lucky and helpful decisions in those early days. Maria, who was still essentially a girl and not yet married herself, and Rosa, really helped me through those first few months of the girls' infancy.

Six days after delivery, and two days after I was released, Mia came home from the hospital, leaving Everest and Lily behind in the hospital nursery. The doctor, I later learned, was mostly concerned about my ability to adjust to motherhood. The hospital had apparently given him the authority to determine the timing of each baby's release, and he thought having all three babies sent home at once would be too much for me, on top of recovering from my C-section surgery. So, Mia was our sole treasure for those first few days. I still have a visual of Mia propped up on top of a huge pile of laundry, like a princess, while Maria folded away. When we went to the hospital five days later to retrieve Everest and Lily, it almost didn't happen. The doctor was not in, and they needed his authorization to release them into our care. Finally, the doctor arrived, and he needed some convincing.

"I'm *fine*," I said to him. "I'm *ready* to handle all three."

He appeared unmoved. "Just a few more days while you adjust I think would be better," he responded.

Oh no! I thought. This can't be happening. "I want them now, Doctor, please. We can handle it. *Pleeease*," I seemed to need to add. After explaining to him that we had an unusual volume of hired assistance at home, he finally relented.

We wheeled our new Triple Decker Stroller (more on that later) into the hospital, and collected our second and third clothed-in-pink treasure babies. Mia came along for the ride, as did Grandma and Grandpa. It was what my husband would refer to as a "red letter day."

Once home, we had new challenges. Lily and Everest looked so alike during those first few weeks that I worried about confusing them. I kept their hospital anklets on them until I was sure I knew who was who. Thankfully Everest's nose was a tiny bit broader than Lily's, so I was able to tell them apart. And Everest also had a habit of sticking out her tongue and waving it from side to side while rolling her eyes, which we adults thought was pretty hilarious.

Maria slept in our spare room and worked all day long on this or that, either cleaning or baby-related, until the dinner dishes were put away.

Rosa came at 10:00 p.m. and left at 6:00 a.m., taking care of all the night feedings, burpings and diaper changing, miraculously leaving Simon and me (and Maria) a full eight-hour window to sleep and literally catch our breath.

It was almost surreal, having triplets and being able to sleep. Perhaps there are some who would choose not to entrust each night's childcare with someone else...but sleep beckoned. I still was recovering from my C-section, and I just gave myself that gift. We had all day long to be together, I reasoned, when it was daylight and I was rested, and that's what we did. Friends would marvel at how calm Simon and I both were, and I have to say, I agree that those were calmer days than the years that followed.

If I hadn't hired those two helpers, Rosa and Maria, I believe I would've had quite a few more out-of-control incidents than just the one I had a few weeks later when I angrily tore off my milk-pumping bra and apparatus... there's really something to be said for having help with just the basics.

One tip, if you want to call it that: try not to have triplets if you can't afford it. When you can pay for help, clothes, diapers, formula and three of everything else without stressing about the cost, it's much more fun than penny pinching each purchase. With us, somehow in the beginning

I didn't feel the strain, but it came later with a vengeance. I guess we knew that kids would be expensive, but who knew we'd be having three? All I can say is, it ain't cheap. So if you think you might be having multiples (or eventually want to get married and have children), word from the now wiser—save up. It's never too soon to start.

Nursing (or Not!)

I had my first experience with anger management, or rather lack thereof, when I did battle with what I referred to as my milk-pumping bra. This special bra had a hole in just the right place to facilitate excreting milk with the aid of an attached tube and pump. The pump squeegeed my breast (yes, squeegeed, no joke), causing the milk to drop into the attached tube and bottle.

It was week three after the girls were born, and Rosa and Maria had their individual systems in place, washing bottles and making formula, so the girls would all have enough to eat and not need to rely upon whatever mother's milk I might produce. Thankfully my doctor was a pragmatist. He believed that nursing is a mother's option, for the mother's enjoyment and bonding experience, and that bottle-feeding is a perfectly suitable alternative for any tired mother not able or willing to let her newborn(s) suckle at her breast. In my case, late to motherhood already, I just needed to give everything a try, and that included nursing.

So I put the nursing bra and pump on my baby registry, and once equipped with all the required hook-ups and apparatus, I gave it my all. I breast fed two babies at once, with some success. This of course required a helper to hand me baby #2, once baby #1 was properly situated. Rosa was handling all the nighttime feedings, and my hope was to pump some milk and store it for her to use at night.

But sadly, my output was lacking. I'd spend fifteen to twenty minutes per sitting, allowing my breast to be squeezed and pulled, generally with only one ounce to show for my labors. I was exhausted and depressed by my poor harvests. At least once I spilled what I had pumped, which left me in tears and more than a little discouraged by the wasted effort. I had some sweet moments of bonding while breastfeeding with each of my girls, but truth was, breastfeeding hurt a little. Also, my happiness was tempered by my concern that my breast wasn't giving adequate milk. Maybe the babies would be left hungry, even after feeding at my breast. That gnawed at me.

I hit the wall one day, struggling with the bra and pump and tubing. My commitment to the venture was flailing. I was exhausted, despite my supposedly full night of sleep. After a screaming bout one evening with no one (it was just me and the pump), I decided that that was it. My kids were going to need to fare well on commercially produced milk. And that was that.

So I suppose that's one of my first real experiences to share…and eight years later I can still consider heeding my own advice: don't try to do it all. I only missed the actual nursing a little bit, because even though it was sweet, at least with the bottle I knew exactly how much food my little angels were getting, which to me was more important than antibodies, right or wrong. And thankfully I had my doctor's blessing, so I skated through that early decision without much guilt, and took the first deep breath of my motherhood.

Taking the Triplets to Hollywood

My timing was perfect. It may have coincided, in fact, with the moment I angrily swore off nursing and breast milk pumping.

Seeking something more fruitful, I reached out to a group I had joined for moral support, the West Los Angeles Mothers of Multiples. I inquired on their online group chat venue, "Has anyone tried doing commercials with their kids?" "Was it successful?" I also wanted to know.

It was 1:00 a.m., a good time it seemed for doing my maternal research. It became a new habit, for some years anyway, working in the middle of the night. In any event, five moms responded within 24 hours, all recommending the same agent. They offered related advice and cautionary encouragement. It could be lucrative, they shared. It could be tedious too, they added.

As it turns out, baby multiples are in high demand with the folks that make commercials and TV shows. Who would've known? I was encouraged, amped up, ready to tackle something new, now that I had given up breast feeding. Why not Hollywood? It could be fun. I was not deterred by any of the cautionary feedback.

So by the time the girls were three weeks old, we had an agent (the recommended one), two upcoming auditions, and shortly thereafter, our first commercial gig. Lily played a prodigy baby on a Cars.com commercial. It was a cute concept. With the assistance of a mechanical arm, Lily (playing a brand new just-born baby named David, and still on the delivery table) appeared to be giving direction to the (stage) doctor, who had supposedly just delivered her from her (stage) mother's womb. We found it humorous that the art department, in an error in judgment, had made the mechanical arm more pudgy than Lily's actual arm. But you couldn't see that on the commercial, so no one was the wiser.

It was a whirlwind, it was easy and fun, and in that same week the girls had their next audition. They went to that audition in style, having been gifted three matching purple corduroy outfits with matching berets and shoes by a close friend. The star of the *The Young & the Restless* fell in love with the girls on the spot, being a hat person herself. Before we even exited CBS's parking lot in West Hollywood, we were given the happy news of having been hired, which led to over thirty episodes of one or the other of the girls playing baby Delia in that show.

When babies are small, they are easy to switch out one for the other. The viewer typically isn't watching that closely and doesn't notice. The babies always (always, always) wear a knit cap, or some other head covering, and they more or less look the same, especially if they are siblings. Studios often hire twins or triplets, because having three baby girls play one infant in a TV series allows the producers to ensure that there aren't film delays associated with a child crying or needing a diaper change, or being in the throes of some other inconvenient bodily need. We used to joke about Mia getting the least airtime, because she was either eating, sleeping or pooping much of the time when there was a need for a baby on set.

There are lots of rules in the industry to protect "the talent," and until the girls were six months old, the producers were limited to using the girls twenty minutes "under the lights" as they call it, and to keeping them at the studio no more than four hours during any given hiring day.

The process of being in show business actually entails quite a bit of sitting around and waiting for one's scene. But my helper and I enjoyed the novelty of being on set, even if much of the time we were simply passing time in a crowded room entertaining the girls and ourselves until we were called to be "on set."

We learned to pack up snacks and other diversions for both the car and the time spent at the studio, and reveled in the subsequent TV airings that we shared with friends and family proudly. The checks didn't hurt either. More rules on that: Jackie Coogan, a child actor who started out in the era of silent films, lost his entire childhood's earnings. His parents spent his entire fortune, leaving him with nothing to show for all his work when he became an adult. Since then, laws have been established to protect children's acting earnings. Now parents have to set up accounts to safeguard no less than 15% of the child's earnings so that they accrue to the child's benefit no matter what. We had bank accounts to set up, and work permits to secure. Had the girls been under thirty days old at the time of their first working engagement, we would have needed the pediatrician's written permission as well.

It was a fun ride, those first two years. We ended up doing three commercials and several TV shows over that period. It was lucrative and also fun, both good motivations for continuing to pursue it. We built up a nest egg that may cover the cost of a year, or maybe even two, of the girls' future college educations. And it gave us a glimpse into the previously mysterious world of television production.

We filmed a TV movie with Jennifer Lopez, two episodes of *Lie to Me*, half a season of *Sons of Anarchy*, two episodes of *CSI*, and a Kay Jewelers commercial. The glamour eventually wore off, especially when we had one episode of a show with an actor, who drove off with Lily in an unsecured car seat in the back of a muscle car when the scene had not called for any live action at all.

Thankfully nothing terrible happened. I was shook up though, and I remember feeling like I didn't receive an apology from the star at all, who just shrugged, perhaps since no accident had occurred. Anyway, in all our experience, that was the only truly unsafe incident we experienced. The studios are generally beyond vigilant about child safety.

The girls' nanny (who doubled as my mother's helper) and I were constant companions during the girls' eighteen-month *The Young & the Restless* stint. We packed bags of snacks, extra formula and diapers, and toys to entertain. We never knew how long we would be waiting in the little room referred to as the "actor's lounge."

One of us would wait at the foot of the stairs while the other would precariously carry the other two up the dozen or so steps, sometimes aided by the stage "handler" or "teacher," other times managing on our own. The "lounge" was nothing more than a small rectangular shaped room. I'd guess it was 8' x 15', and it was filled with couches, porta-cribs, chairs and a changing table. There was barely any floor space, the room was so stuffed with furniture that might be needed for any given age group.

When the girls turned six months, *The Young and the Restless* no longer required all three of them, since at that age the law allows children to be on set for up to two hours under the lights and up to six hours at the studio location. From that point on they only wanted to hire and pay for two actors and not three, so Mia was counted out, given that she had been in fewer episodes than her sisters (a result of her frequent and ill-timed eating, sleeping and pooping, as mentioned above).

On each filming day, the production staff brought in two identical and new outfits for the performance. We needed to have the girls ready in order for just one to take her turn on the set, the second acting as a backup in the event of inconsolable tears or the need for a diaper change requiring a fast replacement. We would dress them in the provided outfits, placing the requisite knitted cap, or hat, on their heads. In theory, the hat made it less obvious that the girls were not identical, since they were playing the same character in the show, Baby Delia. By the time the girls were over a year old, it became pretty obvious to anyone paying attention that they were two separate babies…they didn't even have the same eye color.

Thankfully, even though Everest and Lily clearly no longer looked alike, they were apparently adored by the show's fans, who were willing to forgive their dissimilarity. So, the studio continued to keep them on in the role.

Eventually the girls wailed their protest. They didn't want

62 Balancing Three

to be held by any pretend mommy, daddy, aunt or uncle, no matter how nice they might be. While I had always told myself I'd stop the acting gigs if the girls didn't like it, I was under the spell of the checks that were rolling in, and finally had to be told by one of the show's producers that it just wasn't working out anymore. And that was the end of *The Young and the Restless*, for us anyway. My little actors had become too restless for *The Young and the Restless,* it seemed.

We continued to maintain the girls' work permits until just two years ago, when I finally decided to call it quits. We booked and worked two additional commercials after that first long run of TV work. But mostly it was audition after tiring audition with no callback (second audition) or callbacks with no bookings. There are grueling waits at times for a two-minute audition. So the glamour of the industry comes with a price: you have to be willing to participate in the cattle call, the constant photo and casting website updates, and the disappointment of not being selected after having reworked your afternoon, or your entire day, on a moment's notice, often to no avail.

So it's not for everyone. I kept thinking I'd reached the

point of being ready to give up on the promise of their stardom when a new audition invitation would show up in my email inbox, tempting me again. And off I would go, rearranging our plans, my appointment schedule, and even purchasing new outfits if I thought it might help. And then would come the disappointment...no news. You're not supposed to bother the agent by following up.

"Don't call us, we'll call you," they advise. I'd follow up anyway. I couldn't help myself.

The whole venture could have been on some level the pursuit of an unrealized dream of my own, who knows. But the absence of bookings eventually wore out my waning enthusiasm. I had mixed feelings about it for sure. I certainly didn't like the superficiality of the trade. Our agent had advised us to get caps for our kids' missing teeth, if any, because apparently agents don't like missing teeth. How can they possibly not like the adorableness of missing front teeth? But the promise of good money was intoxicating, and it kept me, and us, in the hunt.

Again and again, I'd begin to consider other options for eventually "passive" income to offset the cost of three future college educations—and then we'd receive yet another audition notice.

Poof! Thoughts of past trials and tribulations would go out the window, memories of past bookings would flash before my eyes, and off we would go. Hope springs eternal, I guess.

When we hit the two year mark of auditions with no bookings, with the girls clearly less than enthused about the prospect of what the auditions entailed (neat hair, tidy outfits, hours in the car, who could blame them?), I decided to pull the plug. No more auditions, no more photo updates. No more clothing purchases because I thought someone else might like "the look," or because the colors or patterns would photograph well. When I changed their audition profiles to "offline," it was with a twinge of regret, but also a sigh of relief. From then on we could be just us, living our own lives, not seeking the approval or endorsement of anyone else. Money would have to find us another way.

How Do You Do It?

During the first few years of our daughters' lives I found myself often anxious and stressed about money. I worked, and worked, investing hours in our business, while our nanny watched the girls. I realized over time that my efforts were too broad, and that I had wasted more than a few hours pursuing business opportunities and clients that just weren't ideal targets for our company's services.

When I finally sat down to consider which of my efforts were translating into tangible results, I realized I needed to make some changes. I was now a mother of three little girls who needed their mama, nanny notwithstanding. And I needed them too. The time was behind me for "doing it all." I couldn't do it all, and more than that, I no longer wanted to. I started dropping my business networking groups like hotcakes, eliminating all but two, and even then being selective as to which events I would attend.

As I freed up my time, I noticed that our business seemed to land the same—or an even greater—volume of business, with less stress and less effort. Our newest clients seemed to be a better fit for us. Feeling validated with my streamlined approach to new business generation, I allowed myself to continue to eliminate any events or business functions that I couldn't clearly tie to signed business contracts.

These days I work from home, and some days I can even put the word "work" in quotes. I love it. My work from home model isn't a fit for everyone, I know, but when someone asks, "How do you do it?" that's part of my answer.

I'm no longer getting dressed to impress every day. I'm not worrying about transporting the files or papers I need from office to home and back. I'm not worrying about driving, parking, walking to, or "starting" to work at any specific time. I just do what needs to be done, when it needs to be done.

Since I've eliminated most of my comings and goings, I've managed to fit my work hours into a finite window of time that also leaves time for me to just be, well, a mom. My home office works for me, even if it's smack in the middle of our family room, and offers me no privacy once the girls are home.

I'm not an efficiency expert, mind you. I'm just happy to have my kids, and hoping to get this parenting thing "right." And if you asked me to define what exactly "getting it right" means to me, the overriding thought that comes to mind is for my daughters to be happy, and well-adjusted to life. I can probably say that I really do have everything I've always wished for. "Ask and ye shall receive." I believe that to be true. So how do I do it, you ask? I just do.

Are They Identical?

We had picked out our baby names before the girls were born (that exercise is a story for another day), so when the girls were born we needed only to decide which girl seemed to best fit which name. Mia had come into my room first after the delivery, and we knew right away that she would be Mia.

Now, of course, most every parent thinks their baby is beautiful, and in the case of our girls, they are all deliciously so. But Mia seems to draw particular attention as being especially pretty, judging from the comments we receive. Even during the gap-toothed years, Mia's features remained arguably perfect—if you don't consider the incongruity of conspicuously missing front baby teeth. Even now, with her big teeth grown in, Mia sports an endearingly funny, wide and sometimes mischievous grin, which is sometimes shielded by her shyness, and hidden behind her fist or arm.

Up until recently, we kept Mia's straight blond hair in bangs. But this required ongoing maintenance, so for the past few years (it seems), we've been painfully growing them out, clipping them to one side or straight back, allowing us to see her pretty little forehead. Usually Mia's hair is in a messy ponytail, messy only because as she moves throughout her day, she often touches her hair, loosening the ponytail and clips. And frequently the long bangs now cover her eyes to the point where she is looking out between strands of long blond hair.

Mia is thin, but not exactly skinny. Often she's got a smudge of lunch still on the side of her pretty mouth, signs of chocolate or the strawberries she loves to eat. The smudges often carry over to the front of her shirt or maybe her pants—in a telltale trail of where her hands have been. Mia favors pink, and typically is attired head to toe in clothes of all shades of that color. She's my beautiful, messy treasure.

Everest is my brown-eyed girl. Everest is the only one with brown eyes, which are a medium, hazel-like shade of brown, and very round in shape. Her eyes are like saucers on her delicate oval face with its ever so slightly pointed chin. Everest has light olive-toned skin, which gets very tanned in the summer, unlike her two sisters.

Everest has light brown hair streaked with blond highlights that any image-conscious adult female would covet. She is thin and muscular and in constant motion, often jumping in excitement, arms in the air, exercising her own personal variation of Jumping Jacks.

Everest's hair is straight, and just below shoulder length. It easily separates from her mom's carefully-created ponytail through the constant motion of her enthusiasm. Everest prefers comfortable clothes that don't inhibit her activity, most often T-shirts with an animal image, given the choice. When Everest sported her own gap-toothed smile, missing her two front teeth, it made her already pretty face even more adorable to me. When she was a baby, her aunt (my sister) nicknamed her Smiley Everest, a nickname we all loved and kept in use for some time.

Everest is thoughtful, her heart-shaped face the most expressive of her sisters, registering surprise, sadness, wonder and excitement with a furrowed brow, a wide downturned mouth, or a big grin. She is engaged with some emotion that registers in her eyes every moment of her day. She is my tenderhearted, beautiful brown-eyed girl.

Lily is the runt of my litter, so to speak. Smaller by nearly a pound at birth, to this day she is a full two inches shorter and three or four pounds lighter than her tallest sister. Lily is petite, determined, and very fair-skinned, with blue, almond shaped eyes that look green at times. Her nose is tiny and perfect, like all her features, except perhaps her ears, which stick out a little.

When Lily was three or four, still innocent in the matters of image, she commented, pointing out that she'd won this particular contest: "I have the biggest ears" (of all her sisters). She hasn't repeated that statement since, so I wonder at times if she's aware that by today's beauty standards, big ears aren't a feature a girl would generally brag about. I haven't brought it up with her; there's no point.

Lily's straight, white blond hair is just below shoulder length. She also seems to have an eye for mixing patterns, and on any given day may be attired with stripes, flowers and solids of more or less similar shades of color, sported with confidence and without reservation. Lily is cute by the observation of one of her classmates, with a ready smile or giggle, and a desire at all times to be "doing" something. Lily also seems to revel in running the show, and is the most independent of all three of the girls. I joke about her being the boss of me when I let her. We think Lily may become a business owner one day.

Happy Preparations

It's just after midnight and I've finally "thunk" myself awake...even after melatonin and an hour's worth of sitcoms. Another of my midnight sessions of busyness, a shift in my pattern since the girls were born.

My day was just too busy, full of completing two Mother's Day projects and a bon voyage dinner for my parents who somehow forgot about the invitation (this is what often happens in one's late 80s, the short-term memory is just not all there)...and this on a day when my most recent mother's helper called in needing a personal day off due to marital problems. I empathized with her. Life wasn't always peaches on the marital front. I'd say "more on that later," but I think that's a subject for my next book.

As you may have already gleaned, I can sometimes operate

like a one-woman machine. I powered through the rest of day. Who needs a helper anyway? I can do it, I coached myself. Now, more than twelve hours later, it's just not easy to switch me off. And a late night writing interlude does not bode well for my intended 8:00 a.m. morning exercise. I wonder if I can just spill out these thoughts quickly and then get to sleep in time to rest up and rally for another day.

Toys keep sounding off in Lily's bedroom, keeping me company, perhaps tripped by my movements as I made my rounds ensuring blankets covered little bodies and lights were turned low. My cat sits on a soft blanket on our loveseat, leaving me my writer's chair for a change. I couldn't turn my mind off this evening, and writing wasn't bringing me its usual solace. Some unpaid bills were weighing on my mind, and sitting still to put my thoughts to rest didn't suit my current mental state.

Funny expression that—"to rest." Putting my thoughts to rest would certainly be a helpful outcome here, although so far unattainable tonight. Is it the thought that needs to rest or the worry that accompanies the thought? I worry whether I did my best, I worry about what remains to be done, and I fret over which are the right words to communicate to people, to helpers, employees and clients. And tonight I'm pondering what most merits saying now, before the thought or memory fades.

So, back to my story...

A fairly major and time-consuming bit of research and purchasing I did before the girls were born were my car and car seats. My husband laughed at how insistent I was on getting a car that had latches on three seats next to each other, so that the infant car seats could fit handily and safely in them. I chose the Honda Pilot, followed a few short years later by the Honda Odyssey minivan. It seems that latches are already out of favor with the safety experts, but this was nearly a decade ago.

We later purchased a narrow profile type of child car seats called Sunshine Radians that allowed me to fit three across in the same row, even in a non-SUV style vehicle. Those car seats were one of the best purchases we made when the girls were little. They used those car seats until a little over a year ago, believe it or not.

It brings to mind that many of the choices I made in those days were aided and abetted by the advice I got from the two Mothers of Multiples groups I joined during my pregnancy. I'm generally not a group person, preferring one-on-one interactions to group activities. But the Mothers of Multiples groups I joined had web pages and member email exchanges that enabled me to bounce many thoughts or questions off a group of women who were either in the process of making the same decisions, or who had already made them. The advice I was able to get, essentially for free, more than paid for the small fee they required for dues. And I did occasionally enjoy the camaraderie of their fellowshp, when I took the time to mingle in person.

Cars and car seats weren't the only matters requiring consideration and purchase in advance of the girls' birth. Walking and sleeping matters also required forethought and consideration. Strollers were first on my list. After contemplating horizontal vs. vertical configurations of triple strollers, we opted for the vertical type (better for getting through doors), and purchased a stroller patented under the name Triple Decker Stroller.

It was a bit on the heavy side, which made getting the frame in and out of the car a challenge, especially with its solid wheels and construction. And it had one design defect in that it needed to be loaded with babies from bottom to top, and then unloaded top to bottom. Should these instructions go unheeded, one would experience the quite undesirable and rather frightening outcome of the entire device tipping backward—with however many babies still in the unit being carried down with it. Thankfully, the two or three times this occurred, my little ones were so small as to be still safely protected in their car seat carriers, which snapped securely into place in the frame. This stroller may no longer be available for purchase, so I'll not elaborate any further. The triplet technology has advanced, I do believe.

Cribs were next on my list. We had prepared a room for the girls to share, not having the luxury (as few would, perhaps) for separate bedrooms for each. The room was not large, measuring 12'x15', and would have been somewhat cramped with three cribs. Luckily I came across a manufacturer offering something called a mini crib, and we purchased three of these, and then debated about the merits of décor vs. function. After four months or more of having Lily and Everest on one side of the room and Mia on the other, we opted eventually to throw fashion to the wind and let the three girls sleep next to each other, a very crowded looking arrangement, but one that made us as parents feel better that one girl wasn't being excluded from the nearby companionship of her sisters. The girls used the cribs until they were able to gingerly jungle gym their way out, and even then for many more months, until we finally filmed their exit down the hall, greeting their new fresh white toddler beds in their place. I was seemingly the only teary-eyed one of the bunch of us. Even my sister commented that I shouldn't get emotional, lest it be catchy.

Bottles and Toilet Training

It already seems a blur, the days and months of the girls drinking formula in bottles. We held onto that for a long time. I wasn't in a hurry to end any particular baby phase... not for them nor for me. We'd made the decision already that we would not be having any more kids, so I wanted to enjoy each stage as much as I could. And what's the rush anyway? The girls would be drinking out of glassware eventually, no matter when they gave up bottles. Why not let them hold onto that apparently comforting "baba" if it made them happy?

When the girls were babies we carried them everywhere in their car seat carriers. More often than not, they would suddenly all be crying for attention, or a bottle, you never knew which. With help, the task of feeding all three went smoothly, but on days with no help, it was a bit of a feat to accomplish. On the days when I had periods of managing the girls on my own, I felt like I was in a race for a prize, the prize being all babies happily sucking away at their bottle and not crying. I had seen advertised, but never did buy, individual bottle stands to prop the bottles in front of their mouths when they were too little to hold the bottles themselves. When I heard about the bottle stands, the idea of a possible choke hazard scared me, and I never did try them out. We propped the bottles up and in their little mouths, with blankets and anything else handy to keep them in place so that the girls could drink without an adult needing to hold the bottle for them. In hindsight it sounds a bit uncaring, but that was our reality. The girls would move their heads from side to side, and eventually used their hands to push the bottles away from their mouths when they'd had enough. The event was a little messy, especially when the bottles ended up sideways, or worse, upside down. But at least the girls were fed and not in danger of choking.

It was the girls' third birthday before we gave up the bottles for good. With the party preparations, the bottles went in the "give-away" pile, and that was that. We gave up diapers at the same time. Our "toilet training," if you want to call it that, happened during the summer months when the girls were two-and-a-half, going on three. They ran around our fenced and private backyard naked, or close to it, and when the accidents occurred, as they did, of course, they were no big deal. It was almost a non-event. Gradually the girls got the gist of the program. If they tinkled, something wet would run down their legs.

I finally took a moment to translate the coupons that came with the family-size boxes of Pampers we had grown accustomed to purchasing, just as we were finishing our last box. The coupons for some inexplicable reason were printed only in Spanish, so I had always just set them aside, not having the presence of mind to study them in the midst of a diaper changing event. My belated efforts caused me to realize that Pampers offered a purchase rewards points program that would have given us purchase discounts on our favorite brand. Oh well, I thought, no point stressing over that one since it was too late to do anything about it anyway. It still hurt though. I didn't even know how much money I could've saved. It just was the principle of the matter. So much for being thrifty and pennywise.

Anyway, there's good news for you if you're expecting, or better yet already have, your own brood of triplets. I'm still standing, right? I've lived to tell about it. I'd venture to say that's evidence that you too can manage triplets, if that's your lucky lot. Or also take in stride whatever life challenges you may face. My triplet daughters are now eight years old. Every six months goes by in a flash. I remember the first year of my daughters' lives, feeling triumphant that I was experiencing each moment so fully, right up until the girls' first birthday, which falls two weeks before Christmas. And then...wham!

The first birthday party was over, and then Chanukah and Christmas came and went, and New Year's (all in two weeks), and suddenly, just like that, the girls were thirteen months old. It caught me off guard.

"Wait," I silently cried. "They just turned one year and I didn't get to breathe that in. Now they're thirteen months old! I'VE MISSED IT!" (They being one year old, that is).

At some point, like me, you may have experienced the sensation that time flies faster than you'd like. A friend in touch with her other worldly senses recently told me that this sensation of time flying has actually been a documented phenomenon, and that the speed of time is actually accelerating. So strap your boots on, Momma.

Finding the Perfect Nanny

I ushered the next nanny candidate into our house as I held one of the babies in my arms. The applicants had begun to blur, and I clung to the hope that this next young woman would somehow resonate as being "the one." Funny, the search for our nanny was not much different than husband hunting.

"I'm Theresa," she said, holding out her hand for me to shake. I shook it, and we stood near the entry awkwardly.

Theresa was a little plump, with long brown hair pulled into a ponytail, a round face, and brown eyes. While we stood talking only a few steps from the front door, Theresa picked up a baby blanket that had fallen to the floor, folding it neatly before putting it down on the couch nearby. I noted the gesture and noticed also my feeling of associated relief.

The small household task spoke to me, as in "this girl can help me."

Our live-in nanny Maria had given us notice the week prior, the notice actually being no notice at all, but instead an apology that she couldn't work for us any longer, having been forbidden to do so by her new spouse. Oh, dear. We didn't dwell on the shame of her predicament, that of having married someone who apparently wanted to be her keeper. We were too shocked by the lack of notice to do more than wish her good luck in her new marriage.

We were in a tailspin for the next two weeks. Dishes had piled up in the sink, along with several undone loads of laundry. We had no ready back-up to fill the gap left by Maria's absence. Any thoughts that I might previously have had such as, "I can do this on my own," immediately flew out of my mind as I dealt with the practicality of three eight-month-old infants in my care during the day without help.

I immersed myself in the selection of potential replacements offered by care.com, an online membership-based employment website. I was happy to locate this online tool, which lessened the pain associated with the process of finding a household helper. The website gives both applicant and employer the opportunity to cite his or her qualifications or requirements, while also noting specific hours of availability or needs as well as salary range requirements. This cut out the time that could otherwise be wasted, vetting candidates who either weren't available the days or hours we needed, or perhaps with salary requirements we couldn't afford.

I had isolated a handful of candidates to interview, hoping that one of them would fit the bill and take the position, so that our little household could resume some semblance of normalcy.

"Let me show you around," I said, and I walked Theresa through our now rather untidy house.

Before the interview was over, Theresa had held one of the girls, changed the diaper of another, prepared a bottle of baby formula, and sat on the floor with a third baby as I looked on, surveying the calmness of her interaction with my little ones. I didn't spend much time deliberating. Theresa started work with us the next day.

I'm sitting now at my desk in our kitchen and family room, reflecting back on the times I sat at this very desk, doing my "work" from home. I can recall Theresa sitting on the floor nearby, entertaining the girls. At that time they were not yet walking. I can remember thinking, "I'm not needed here."

Everything was under control, expertly managed by my new helper who did not need my assistance, although I did need hers. Theresa never quite became my friend during the time of her employ. She was reserved, diligent, and did her job, without being chatty or in need of my company or assistance. She did it all. Bottles were washed and filled, laundry folded and put away, girls were content, entertained and often giggling. She was most definitely "a keeper."

Theresa happened to be handy, or at least claimed to be so. "I can put that together for you," she announced one day, as I brought home a new piece of assemble-it-yourself furniture from Target.

Theresa put that together, as well as the girls' outdoor playhouse, and even an outdoor shower I had purchased from World Market. Somehow there were always parts left over. The shower never did function. Simon said something was installed upside down. Oh well, the offer to assemble it had seemed like a good idea at the time.

Theresa left us after three fast years. When she called to

give her notice, she apologized for taking an unexpected job offer.

"You're not going to need me full-time next year," she said, anticipating in advance our lessening need once the girls began preschool.

My later hiring experiences looking for part-time help did not go quite as smoothly as that earliest effort. Something often was off, either the person's demeanor (not happy enough), or tidiness (not tidy enough) or any other number of deficiencies that made them an imperfect and therefore temporary fit. I realized belatedly that our family had been quite blessed to so easily find someone who surely loved our daughters, and who cared for them just as we did, and in many ways even better. We made a keepsake of a photo frame with Theresa's handprint and photo in it, hoping to dull the pain of the girls' separation from the nanny they had grown to love. But time quickly passed, and the keepsake was not long after assigned a place hidden away on the bedroom closet shelf.

Theresa has become a distant memory to the girls. She's come over to babysit from time to time, her own schedule full now that she has grandchildren of her own to mind. The girls didn't really seem to recognize her the last time she visited. My eyes tear up as I think about all the moments we shared as a family unit back then, Theresa expertly managing whatever needed managing, me sometimes feeling superfluous to the harmony she created with my three. I needed her, and I knew it. She was the professional, having raised three kids of her own. I was the onlooker, ultimately responsible, but definitely an "extra" helper when she was in charge.

I sigh, thinking fondly and wistfully of those early days. The baby years are well behind us now. The sun inexorably beats down on us outside, another scorching November day here in Southern California. On my desk sit three ceramic tiles with the girls' handprints, and three flower pens in decorated ceramic pots, both projects from elementary school. The girls are in their room, watching a video on their Chromebook. It's 11:11 a.m. on a Sunday, definitely time to engage them in something other than TV time. Time to get myself cleaned up and out of my own version of PJs—T-shirt and sweatpants.

I sigh again, breathing deeply this time. Time marches on.

Mommy and Me Activities
Parenting Classes

There are just some things about pregnancy and motherhood that are different with triplets. As I shared, mine was not a relaxing pregnancy boasting marvelous hair and manicured nails. I was nervous and would have chewed my nails if that were my habit (thankfully not), and my hair didn't look any different at all as I recall, except perhaps flat in the back due to so much bed rest.

Mommy and Me activities was another outing I tried, and tried to enjoy, and did enjoy in parts, of course. Who doesn't enjoy a baby or toddler in a soft gym setting, learning to use their precious and adorable little bodies? We went to our local My Gym, a safely-padded setting where adults and toddlers alike wore socks and no shoes. The toddlers got to know the strength in their bodies by climbing, jumping, and playing in the indoor gym, until the group activities would begin. We'd sit in a circle, tapping our hands and feet to the rhythms of the song, until eventually a song would require the mommy and child to partner up. There I was, with three sets of expectant eyes on me.

"Choose me!" "Choose me!" their eyes beckoned, yet only one could be chosen—for that particular song, anyway. And my happiness was interrupted with feeling badly for the two left without a partner. Fortunately, the instructor or the assistant instructor typically observed our distress and jumped in to assist with at least one. And with a little luck there were usually enough helpers in the vicinity ready and willing to come to the rescue for my third.

We eventually cancelled our My Gym membership, in large part due to my feelings of inadequacy. It's not that I judged myself for it. I just wanted to do an activity that didn't give me any heart pangs.

It may have been while attending a My Gym class that I met a mom who told me about a local parenting class, and months and months later I finally looked into it and then enrolled. Calling the classes "parenting classes" seemed a bit of a misnomer, because at least the ones I attended encouraged and expected the parents to bring their child with them. The classes were conducted with a morning schedule very much like that of a pre-school, including a morning full of activities for the children. It essentially was a pre-school for toddlers with a parent in the immediate vicinity. No separation anxiety to contend with....not yet, at least. The schedule included a 20-30 minute parenting lesson, held while the kids played nearby. We covered the gamut: potty training, dental hygiene for toddlers, temper tantrums, etc. Often the group exchange was as valuable as the instruction itself.

Attending these classes turned out to be a very helpful stage not only in my parenting, but more importantly, in my children's development (the term "child development" is used a lot I've learned). After taking the girls to these parenting classes once or twice a week for two years or so, they were ready, more or less, to handle a pre-school drop-off program. Sometimes it helps to be friendly. You just never know where or when that next jewel of information is going to come from.

One Room or Three?

We bought our house pre-kids. At 1,800 square feet, it's modest in size for a family of five. It caught our eye with its built-in pool and oversized backyard, which we thought would not only be great for us, but would also most certainly be great for kids, once they were in the picture. Even more enticing was our thought of eventually adding on and building a larger house, if we were ever so inclined. At three small bedrooms with one and three quarter baths, the house seemed appropriately-sized for a middle-aged couple still intending to have kids. We wouldn't end up with more than one or two at our age...or so we thought.

We bought our home in Pasadena, California—a city commonly noted for a less than desirable public school system, this being a result of the preference of the by-and-large wealthy families who lived there to send their children to private schools. The low enrollment had once upon a time caused the school district to introduce busing from less affluent areas, which brought a lower socio-economic class into the student body, thereby reinforcing the tendency of the wealthier families to send their kids to private schools.

We didn't worry the point much at the time of our purchase. The cost of a private school education for one, or if we were lucky two, kids, was one we thought we could manage. Or when the time came we could always move.

So, here we were a few short years later, with triplets on our hands, in a small three-bedroom house in Pasadena.

Having essentially been an only child from the age of ten, when my much older siblings left the household, the idea of our girls having 24/7 companionship by sharing a bedroom seemed ideal to me. And given that they were three girls, there would be no gender separation requirements, even down the line.

I figured we could always plan for separate bedrooms in the future, should we ever expand the house (an ongoing household conversation, with no observable progress), or relocate. When we eventually graduated to three toddler beds, these took up more room than the cribs, but we still managed to fit them all in the one room.

Over the years, our third bedroom has morphed from spare bedroom to home office and back to spare bedroom. Prompted by our daughters' school's entreaty to its parents, when the girls entered kindergarten we volunteered to accommodate a foreign-born school intern who needed a short-term housing arrangement. When the intern's stay ended, leaving the room empty and up for grabs, I made the incorrect assumption that it would be mine for the taking. And I imagined taking pleasure in some late night reading without disturbing my exceptionally light-sleeping husband who awakened at the slightest movement on my part.

But before I had a chance to even glance at the empty closet with an eye toward placing some things of my own within it, Lily had begun moving her belongings over, one drawer at a time, saying she wanted to sleep in the big twin bed "that night," which turned into two, and then suddenly it had become Lily's room and not mine.

I chuckled to myself, realizing that the move did eliminate some of the clutter from having three girls crammed into one small room, which was further restricted in the placement of furniture by three windows and a ceiling fan (not exactly ideal dimensions for bunk bed furniture).

I recently asked Everest if she'd like her own bedroom when the time comes that we do expand our house. She gave the question a moment of contemplation, and then said, "Yes. I'd like my own bedroom. With Mia."

I guess these things have a way of sorting themselves out.

Getting Ready for Pre-school

Pre-school! It was time. The girls were ready, I thought (I hoped) and talking with the moms in my parenting class made me realize that there was no time to waste. We needed to begin researching the options that were available, or possibly miss out on our first choice. You snooze, you lose, I was told; these spots fill up fast.

I learned that a local moms' group puts on an annual pre-school fair, held at the Pasadena City College Auditorium. We loaded the girls, their bottles and burp cloths, extra diapers, and the triplet stroller, in our still-new Honda Pilot. Upon arrival, we found the auditorium full to capacity with literally dozens of local pre-schools, all pitching their programs. We attracted a lot of attention there—which we did pretty much everywhere we went—our long stroller with its pink fabric-lined car seats clipped into place, and three pretty towheads with big eyes looking around, bottles in hand.

We made the rounds through the throngs, as best we could with our long, somewhat unwieldly, baby-filled vehicle. And when we left, I had an armload of brochures describing over a dozen local school programs which were all options to consider. I began the process of visiting the preschools, and applied to one cute neighborhood colonial-style school (aptly named "Colonial House") just to have one application in, and hopefully at least one option available, to our three. So many choices, so many different styles of schools, even at such a young age. Including an option of co-ops, which required significant parent volunteer work to reduce the tuition vs. the cost of a traditional pre-school program.

"You probably shouldn't apply here," a parent at one popular co-op suggested. "There's virtually no chance of three spots being available."

That made things easier for me. The idea of contributing the requisite number of volunteer hours, times three, was already off-putting.

I continued my touring, eliminating possible contenders

one after another for various reasons: one too far, one having too heavy a bleach smell, one too close to the freeway, one too expensive, et cetera, et cetera.

I had thought being a working person was a challenge... and then I became a parent. I was shocked with the realization that this parenting business, steering our children in what I hoped was the right direction, faced us with so many difficult daily decisions to make, and funds to commit. The decisions were hard—for me at least—perhaps due to my aforementioned perfectionistic tendencies. How can one possibly make a decision if one always fears making the wrong one?

The girls ended up attending their first drop-off pre-school at the very first school I had seen (yes, Colonial House). The sweet, white colonial-style traditional house with its deep red-colored front door had been converted to a pre-school. The small rooms were all cheerfully decorated, and its tidy and compact backyard contained clean and new-looking play equipment. I was comforted knowing that the girls would be in a healthy and cute surrounding for their first few hours apart from their momma, from their daddy, and from their now-beloved nanny, Theresa.

I decided to overlook this cute school's one small imperfection—its utter lack of parking. The structure had previously been used as a residence, which meant that there was only one on-site parking space. The only option for us parents was to park our vehicles in the closest neighborhood spot we could find, and to walk our child(ren) the rest of the way. For families with one child, and perhaps another baby in tow, this was somewhat inconvenient. For us, since generally only one of us dropped off the girls (without any helper), parking, unloading, and getting the girls safely to the sidewalk and then to the front door of the school wasn't easy. And that's an understatement.

At each drop-off, I secretly coveted the one and only on-site parking spot. It was for some reason specifically and inexplicably marked "off limits" as further indicated by a red NO PARKING sign. The spot, we later learned, after months of bringing the girls to and fro, was reserved for one sole winning bidder during the school's upcoming fall fundraiser.

My husband and I agreed, prior to the evening event, that this parking space was a necessity for our family. We needed to safely unload our toddler girls away from the street.

Something could too easily go wrong, trying to unload, curbside, three then three-year-old girls. We vowed that no one would outbid us during that auction—come hell or high water. We made one oversight, however, in our preparations for the evening. We forgot to discuss which one of us would be in charge of the bidding. We enthusiastically outbid one another to get it, me from the front, and him from the back of the crowded room. It was all for a good cause, we laughed, recognizing the irony of the still desirable outcome. What's an extra $100 or $200? It goes fast...

The Tooth Fairy

Lily had lost another tooth. She was seven years old at this time, and the precious and valuable tooth was safely held within a plastic tooth charm suspended by a plastic necklace string that was provided by the school office during the day.

"How do you spell 'phone'?" she asked, as we were driving home from school that day.

"P-h-o-n-e," I intoned.

"How do you spell 'number'?" she asked next. I spelled that out for her, too.

It wasn't until late that night, when wearing my tooth fairy wings, that I found her note.

"Dear Tooth Fairy," it read. "My name is Lily. I lost my tooth tday. Plees rite me back."

There were two signature lines drawn below her note with

instructions for the tooth fairy to "Put your phone number here."

I stifled a chuckle. What to say? Fairies don't have phones, the tooth fairy replied. At least that's what Lily reported back in the morning, counting the coins and dollar bills that the tooth fairy had left behind as a gift for the newly lost tooth. She seemed disappointed, but was taking the news in stride, seemingly more interested in the collection of money that was expanding in her piggy bank that would eventually enable her to make a trip to the store to buy an item of her choice.

"Is the Tooth Fairy real?" Mia asked, a few days later.

I put on the expression I used when I wasn't sure how to respond to a question. It's supposed to look thoughtful, like I'm considering the possibilities. I'm not sure if I actually responded. I might have finally said, "I don't know. I think so."

It's April now and the end of the school year is nearly upon us. Before we know it, December will be upon us, bringing with it another triple birthday. Time rolls swiftly past, with my attempts at perfect parenting sometimes getting disrupted by the rigors of daily life and the demands of making a living. I know and feel that the girls' childhood is a fleeting thing, and warn myself not to miss these precious moments before they are past. The days of Santa Claus, the Tooth Fairy, the Easter Bunny...I know they don't last forever. The girls aren't babies anymore. Lily and Everest can read on their own. And soon even Mia won't need me to read to her at night. Thankfully that day hasn't arrived yet.

I scan the trees that make up the view outside my kitchen window and think about the milestones ahead. There will be new subjects to learn, new activities to try, new places to visit, and new friends to make. The overcast sky outside will soon be replaced by summer's sunny days, when picnics at the beach will mark the season.

I know my job as a mother has many years ahead, and there is no need to be wistful like the empty nesters whose children have left home. But still I hold onto this time in my mind, hoping to cement a memory or two, while looking forward to the next time I give one of my daughters a nose-on-nose "kiss," a hug that is reciprocated, or kneel down to wipe away an errant tear. My own eyes fill as I contemplate my heart so full, knowing that it is each and every moment that I will cherish, from now until forever.

Daddy

"Daddy's home!" Lily sang, as we pulled into our driveway.

We had just finished the fifteen-minute drive home from school. Three backpacks and a bag of snacks filled my front passenger seat and floor area, ready now to be unloaded by someone. Hopefully the girls would do it, I thought optimistically. More likely you'll be doing it yourself, I responded back to that thought, or with luck our new housekeeper, Ramona, will pitch in. Getting the girls to be responsible for their own belongings was a work in progress. Simon's family-sized Tahoe was parked curbside, leaving me room to pull in first so that his car could be positioned in the rear of mine, ready to take the girls back to school again tomorrow morning.

The girls grunted and groaned as they unbuckled and left the vehicle, forgetting to take their backpacks as I had predicted they might. Play time awaited them, and they ran through the rear door of our house, immediately immersing themselves in a new activity of their own choosing. Simon is sitting on the couch, working, his laptop aptly located on his lap, something he does on occasional afternoons.

"How was your day?" he calls out, trying to get one of the girls' attention without getting up. "Hey! I asked you a question!" he calls again, as the girls ignore him while they busy themselves in their rooms with who knows what.

I tease Simon about his "couch parenting," sometimes remarking that my own parenting is usually evidenced by action after action, and rarely in a seated position. I guess that I forgot to discuss our respective views on parenting techniques during my 40 questions when I had the chance. As Simon often jokes, it's *so* hard to do everything right.

Simon is playful and quick to laugh, at least when it comes to his three young daughters, who vie for his attention just as they do mine. During the summer, Simon will use his strength in our backyard pool to throw each girl in turn high into the air so that she falls with a big splash and comes up for air asking for more… "Again!" until he begs exhaustion, and finally says, "No more, that's it. Daddy needs a break."

And when he's absent it's more than duly noted, as in "Where's Daddy?" or "When will Daddy be home?" questions I can readily answer with most often "at work," the occasional "playing golf" or "should be soon now."

Simon likes candy too, and will relish a trip to the candy store where he picks out Abba Zabbas or other treats from his own childhood while his girls race around him making their own candy selections. Simon can and will readily put up a tent, and also make a campfire during our occasional camping trips. Simon will buy a golf cart, just for fun, and take us trick-or-treating in it around the block, making us the sensation of our neighborhood.

And Simon barbeques the main dish of our dinners more often than not, be it a barbequed pork chop, or chicken breast or red meat of some variety, attempting to cook it just right so that each of his girls, Mommy included, is happy with the exact tenderness and spice of the final cut.

Simon's latest nightly routine is to give each of his daughters' back a scratch, and he playfully refers to his fingers approaching: "the little man's coming." The girls have become so accustomed to this daily dose of their Daddy's attention that it's become nearly a prerequisite to sleep.

"Daddy! I need my backscratch..." they call to him expectantly. When I look in on the girls at bedtime from our hallway I see Simon sprawled on a bed, leaving barely enough room for its occupant.

"Pleasant dreams," I say, this being the nightly saying of my own childhood. I smile and leave the foursome be, happy that each knows by these paternal attentions that her Daddy loves her, way more than just a little.

So if I don't give adequate voice to the role my other half plays in our household, my husband's presence and contribution are, without question, the final piece to the jigsaw puzzle that makes up our family life. Without him, life just would not be complete.

It's Time for Momma to Take a Break

"I'm not talking to anybody right now. I want a little tiny, tiny, tiny bit of privacy. Go away!" I say to Child #1 from the shower—my first minute alone since 8 a.m. It's after noon and my first shower of the day.

Child # 2 calls, "Mom?"

I yell out in response, "I need a few minutes of privacy. Not now!"

"Mom?" calls Child # 3. She also somehow "needs" me just then.

"Give me a few minutes. Please!" I answer testily.

It's 3:33 p.m. and we haven't done much today. This is a rare gloomy and cloudy day here in Southern California, where the sun shines so many days of the year that we have to ration our water. I say we've done nearly nothing, except as I consider it, I realize we have in fact had an outing to IHOP this morning for a pancake and egg breakfast, and this afternoon made lemon poppy seed cookies from scratch, the aftermath of which is still sitting in my kitchen sink awaiting cleanup.

I guess it feels like we've done almost nothing because I indulged myself in a daytime movie, something I seldom do except if I'm feeling really poorly, which today I'm not; and also because I've allowed the girls to watch *My Little Pony* for what seems like hours today, savoring the peace and quiet of not having to manage their entertainment.

My husband and I are contemplating the dinner options. Do we stay in and prepare food and then wash and put dishes away, or do we spend money on an outing? Dinner out feels like the easier choice today. Our most recently hired household helper, who provides us a mix of cleaning and babysitting services, now affords us the opportunity to have weeknight date nights out. We had already treated ourselves to several dinners out this week, just the two of us. We had to begin questioning the apparent lack of restraint on our spending. Note to self: make time to work on a monthly family budget.

Tomorrow is Mother's Day, and I've prepared a list of what I'd like to do. This also includes what I'd like *not* to be responsible for doing. Simon's gone out to buy hardware (a frequent weekend item on his own "to do" list, (there always seems to be something that needs fixing) and groceries, already anticipating that tomorrow is going to be my day.

My list for tomorrow consists of nothing, not even a massage, because what seems appealing to me these days is to do more of nothing, and less running around.

I've done my share of exposing the girls to practically every activity we can think of that might be fun, or healthy to try (more on that later), and now Momma needs a break. And interestingly enough, the girls seem to need one too, often favoring staying home to running around town. I compare myself to friends with only one child who seem to go somewhere new every single day, and I just can't manage that, nor do I want to. There are too many point-of-purchase opportunities occurring during every outing, times three, and the pressure is on me to be a generous mom, not too tight with the funds, but also to draw the line so the girls can learn restraint and not think that absolutely everything is available just for the asking.

It's actually quite exhausting. And the exhaustion I feel in the midst of these excursions may not even relate to the physical aspect of walking a two-mile path at the zoo, or chasing the girls around the playground, or any other activity that on the surface seems easy and harmless enough from an energy-expenditure stand point. I seem to be in a "let's make things easy" mood today...hence, the lemon poppy seed baking hour. Not as tasty as store-bought, alas, but still good solid, homemaking fun. And paired with an afternoon cup of coffee, the treat of that lemon poppy seed muffin, my personal favorite, was a short and welcome break for Momma too.

Managing Time

My mind is so accustomed to running, and to thinking about what needs to get done—perhaps not unlike other mothers—that I've forgotten how to slow down, and how to let my mind shut down. It's now 12:10 a.m., and I'm too awake to drift off to sleep. It happens from time to time that I miss my window of sleepiness, and my eyes are open. I need to get up and write, or read, as I'm no longer ready to rest. Eventually I'll get out of bed and get to doing something else. Tonight I had settled in for some TV time, but hadn't yet brushed my teeth. And as soon as I got up to do that, I was awake, and that was that. No amount of my nightly dose of sublingual melatonin was going to put me down for the night.

As I mentioned earlier, my husband and I run a construction

company for a living. It has its rewarding moments and fun times too. My role in the company is primarily sales. I look for new business, and with that in mind there's always someone to call and someone to see. And as an owner, I'm also responsible for our success and well-being.

I've noticed that raising my triplets has a lot of parallels to my role in our business; running the household is like running a small business in many ways. There are just littler people to manage, with their various and sundry expectations—plus my husband's own needs and expectations—all while working within a budget. And getting three eight year olds to agree on an activity, or what we are doing for the day, or weekend, etc., I have to say...it puts my sales skills to the test.

The household is essentially my responsibility, much as I try to pass off aspects of it to my husband. These days some couples have a modern division of responsibility, as in fifty-fifty, but my husband and I both grew up in traditional households with the mom as housewife, and so in our relationship, I would objectively say that I manage the household.

And there are days when I simply do not stop moving. As

one example, I frequently eat standing up. I don't advocate this, mind you, it's just become a matter of convenience. I choose not to read the newspaper any more (no time), and when I'm reading a book, it's usually not in the middle of my day. So, a solitary meal is often something that I'm fitting in between whatever else that needs doing. I have to remind myself to take the time to enjoy my food. I've heard that the nutritional value of the foods we consume is enhanced when one appreciates one's food. Standing while eating is a bad habit I seem to have gotten into during my motherhood.

When I was in my twenties, I rented a bedroom in a three-bedroom house in West Los Angeles. The owner was a divorced and single 50-year-old mom with a teenage daughter. To help her cover her mortgage, she had taken in me and another female renter as roommates. I remember noticing that she had an odd habit of eating standing up at the counter. She said it was because of her bad back. She was more comfortable standing than sitting, even for a meal.

And here I am... "ahem" years later, and what do I do? I eat my breakfast standing, almost every single day. The good news is that lately I've managed to actually make myself a hot breakfast, and also to make time to eat it, an improvement over a year ago, when I would be so engaged in the business of taking care of my family that I would literally forget to eat. I used to hear my stomach growling mid-morning on the way to a meeting, and only then realize that I hadn't taken the time to eat. I hadn't remembered to take care of my own basic needs.

I've become engrossed in this "business" of taking care of my triplets. And this venture typically extends to taking care of my husband while I'm taking care of my triplets. Maybe this isn't so unusual. And in the course of taking care of my family, I've noticed that I'm in constant motion. You'd think after all that motion I'd be thin, but alas....

On Friday, my husband and I decided we would have a meal out, just the two of us. We planned to take the girls to a drop-off babysitting program near a restaurant we had in mind. I made a 6 p.m. babysitting reservation at this center aptly named Kids Klub. I had picked up the girls from their after-school program at 4:15 p.m. and sat while they played in the school playground for a while, chatting with another mom. We were home by 5:15 p.m., which should've allowed time to relax for just a few minutes before heading out again.

But suddenly the girls' neighborhood friend from across the street was in our house with her bathing suit on and a towel around her waist. Had I missed something? It was over 90 degrees outside, another unexpectedly warm California fall day. The girls wanted to take a dip in the pool with their friend. I have to admit, I've noticed many of my mothering decisions are made out of guilt. How could I not let them enjoy a break from the terrible heat?

"OK," I said, "but only a few minutes of swim time, because we're going out."

Check out how I managed the next 45 minutes:

5:25 p.m.: bathing suits on—girls jump in the pool (them, not me)

5:45 p.m.: girls in the bath, friend goes home, I wash hair of two girls (third one, little Miss Independent Lily, does it herself, thank G-d!)

6:00 p.m.: brush the hair of the two who need help, get them into their shoes, send the husband and the kids out the door to buckle up in the car while I change my clothes quickly and join them (my husband has already backed out of the driveway so that I am literally getting into the car in the street), and... we're on our way!

6:15 p.m.: arrive at babysitting drop-off center

6:30 p.m.: go to restaurant for dinner and alone time

8:25 p.m.: pick up girls and head home

Sound relaxing? And I wonder why I sometimes have difficulty falling asleep.

Out of Control

I was out of control. My patience had long ago waned, and had turned into anger and frustration. Apparently I was unable to communicate with my daughter. I had sent her to her room as a consequence of her not listening to one or another of my requests. I don't even remember the specifics. I couldn't cool down, and I took it out on her.

To give proper background and perspective to the sequence of events leading up to my offense, and in vain defense of my actions, it bears mentioning that my girls, as a group, have adopted a pattern, over the past several months in particular, of not listening very well. More accurately, they wait to respond to a request until the instruction has been repeated two or three times, this most often causing, by that third time, for the instructing voice to be raised in both pitch and volume.

I could blame our most recent babysitter, who in Simon's opinion definitely enabled this habit by repeating her requests, over and over again, but my parenting is weak in this particular area too. So between her weakness and mine, the girls' new habit has solidified. My husband has pointed out that I contribute to the problem by also routinely repeating my requests without insisting on immediate compliance, or meting out proper and associated punishment in the absence thereof. Punishment could be a "time out," or no dessert for a day, or two, or the unthinkable these days, no "devices."

The early afternoon had been full of pleasure in the camaraderie and company of new mom acquaintances from the girls' language immersion school while mingling at pick up time. These were intelligent and interesting women with whom I felt an immediate kinship. My children and theirs had played happily and independently nearby.

But my mood changed when we returned home, later than our typical dinnertime. The "pork" that my husband had placed in the oven during my absence and at my request, was in fact not perfectly roasted pork at all. Simon had inadvertently cooked some chicken that was also in the fridge, and these were now two clearly over-cooked chicken breasts. I found them sitting on a crispy baking pan on the middle rack of the still warm oven. It was an honest mistake—the chicken and pork looked nearly the same in their individual Ziplock bags in the fridge, marinating in the same colored juice. But chicken doesn't need an hour plus of cooking as the pork would have required, and these two crispy and blackened breasts that I found still cooking away in the oven now represented the less than appealing main dish of our dinner.

In my perception, with my return to the house, the baton had been passed back to me. It now rested on my shoulders to salvage and serve this dried-out dinner and, before or after, to manage bath time for our three young girls. The pleasant glow that I had felt in the company of the women quite suddenly evaporated. Unfolded clean laundry lay in an unkempt pile on top of the dryer, rebuking me to address it, another unfinished task left over from earlier in the day. This was the last of my priorities.

This evening, the offense of the girls not listening to me drew my ire, coupled as it was with the recording in my mind of my husband's disapproval of my tolerance of their habit. Adding strain and stress on my psyche was the housework remaining to be done and the foiled dinner plans. So Mia's not listening simply tested my nerves and patience beyond the breaking point.

As the moments of her time-out ticked by, I relaxed. The irritation of the conflict settled and receded. The time-out was as much for me as for her, it seemed. I placed cold cherry tomatoes, sweet colored peppers, and some leftover reheated pasta in bowls on the table that the girls had helped me set, along with the chicken that my husband had cut into bite-sized pieces for the kids. Dinner was now ready, such as it was.

I entered Mia's room, feeling love and gentleness. "Dinner's ready, Mia."

She was lying in bed, under the covers, protected, with her head and face exposed—a typical time-out posture for her.

"You need to listen to me, you know," I added, almost as an afterthought.

I turned and walked out of her room and into the hallway. By all appearances Mia had heard my words, but her body did not register a reaction or move at all.

My cool and kindness were short-lived. I turned back, seeing that there was no response to my announcement.

"Go!" I said loudly, pulling her out of her bed. My voice is ordinarily a mid-pitch, not high, not low, but it drops to a low alto when I'm angry or when I'm attempting to assert my authority. "Go eat your dinner!" I yelled.

I was mad. Mad at her for not listening, mad at the workload, mad at the messed up dinner, and mad at the lateness of the hour.

My angry and rough push came next, sending her to the floor. She was unhurt, thankfully. I immediately felt regret; I hadn't meant to do that. Oh boy, I thought. Could've handled that better.

Mia got up and sniffled as she walked toward the kitchen. I didn't apologize for pushing her, which I could've done. Should've done. The sniffles turned into tears, predictably, as she sat at the table where everyone else was already seated. Her zero-tolerance father waited less than thirty seconds before sending her back to her room for crying at the table. Insult added to injury...oh dear.

"Use your words," we would admonish. "Crying at the table is not okay." That was our rule.

Right or wrong, Simon rarely ever objects to my parenting methods. We've both been frustrated more than occasionally by the girls not minding us. I think he knew intuitively that this was the root of the current upset. Lily and Everest sat quietly, perhaps not wishing to disturb the mood any further.

The four of us ate silently while waiting through the moments of Mia's newest time out. When she came back into the kitchen, ready for her dinner, quietly, no longer crying, the incident was over. Hunger and the desire for harmony took priority for us all, it seemed.

The girls ate the chicken and cold vegetables with a healthy appetite. We finished our meal without any further upsets. All three girls dutifully collaborated in the task of bringing the dishes to the sink for cleaning. They contentedly munched their chosen desserts, the happy result of consuming sufficient quantities of protein as to warrant the treat.

Tooth brushing and bath time unfolded without a hitch, with more exhibited cooperation (was it related to the earlier time outs, I wondered?) and finally we had three girls in pajamas, hair combed, and all apparently ready for bed.

We were huddled in Lily's room, and Lily had picked out

a Cinderella story for me to read. I laid back on the pillow on her narrow twin bed, while the three crowded around my pillow, Everest and Mia standing, Lily lying tightly beside me on the twin bed. The story was about Cinderella competing in a show with her favorite horse named Frau. Together they won the top ribbon.

We all stayed put as I opened the second book—this one Mia's choice. It was a story about a girl borrowing and using up her friend's pink, white and red paint. It was about friendship and forgiveness. Ironically perfect. I read "The End" and said, rising, "That's enough for tonight, girls. I'll read Everest's story next time."

Once in bed the three drifted off to sleep quickly, dreaming perhaps, I hoped, of something happy like Cinderella, horses, ribbons, or the color pink.

I climbed into my own bed to take in a TV show or two. She forgives me, I thought to myself, knowing my little one well by now. You're a shit, I thought further, about myself, knowing my actions and reactions did not represent me well, nor were they ones that modeled good or decent behavior on anyone's part.

Out of control, I thought regretfully, simply out of control.

Are We Having Fun Yet?

My daughter Lily asked me one day, "Is it fun having children?"

It was an unexpected question. I had to stop and think before I answered it. Why was she asking me that, I wondered? Had I said or done something that prompted it? I thought back over the past several minutes. I hadn't yelled at anyone, or been short tempered. Whew! I exhaled, glad that my rush to self-reproach was unfounded.

"Yes. It's fun having children," I answered. There may have been a twinge of uncertainty in my voice.

Lily's question continued to pop back in my mind in the days and months that followed. I suddenly wanted to get to the root of my answer, and really identify what it was, in fact, that made having children fun. I certainly could easily identify all the labors of it—extra laundry, more dishes to wash, the seemingly endless task of a house that needed tidying. Oddly and to my chagrin, when I looked for the clear examples of times that I would call good old-fashioned fun, I noticed I couldn't quite categorize them as fun, as what came to mind instead were the responsibilities they represented to me. I took up the question on a case-by-case basis.

Going to the zoo...was that fun? Not so much. Too much walking!

Beach...fun? That was clear "yes," but I like the beach no matter what. So I couldn't specifically state that this was a fun that was related to having kids with me. I just happen to love the sand beneath my toes.

So what was it exactly?

I continued to reflect on Lily's question. I spent some time considering what it was that *did* bring me joy, or that *did* sound like fun to me:

- Time spent together as a family (OK, so *that* at least included the girls.)
- Listening to music
- Singing

- Time alone reading or writing
- Swimming (fun with or without the girls. Perhaps more fun with. Phew! Another one.)
- Dancing

Then, I thought about the things related to parenting that were not especially fun for me:

- Rethinking my decisions. Admittedly, this one of my areas of weakness. I do tend to overthink and rethink decisions I've already made. "Did I make the right one?" I often ask myself. This tendency has caused me more than one sleepless night.
- Choices relating to activity vs. down time for the girls. Speaking of which, they are at the moment watching *Puppy Dog Pals* on TV in the other room, in between homework practice drills I administer. Today is a day at home, and I'm good with that. But other days I wrestle with how much stimulation with new activities is important vs. the cost, time and energy to make it happen. Today I have no guilt over my choice, thank goodness.
- Choices relating to money. I hate this one. It impacts

everything. That un-delicious task of maintaining a budget. Camp or no camp? Help around the house or less help around the house? Disneyland or something less pricey? I don't enjoy pondering those choices.

- Too much housework. There are times when it's all I can do to stay on top of everything. And it definitely makes a difference how much help you have. We've run the gamut, from live-in full-time help—with the added services of a nighttime nanny during the girls' infancy—to almost no help, other than occasional babysitting. And everything in between. I've struggled with finding the right fit. My desire to spend less money sometimes gets in the way of making the ideal hiring choice relative to our family's needs. My desire for privacy in my home has also prevented me at times from engaging outside assistance.

As I reflect back, I realize that the "fun" in my life, and our lives, is yet another balance that is largely up to me to strike. Some days I do it well, and others not so much. The "having fun" quotient varies from day to day and week to week. Some days "fun" is a reward for all the chores having been completed, the homework done, and a house that's tidy enough, by most people's standards.

Lately, we've gotten into our own little rhythm. Recently, and not for the first time, we cut back on outside assistance. I've picked up the slack, and Simon too, to bridge the gap, and thankfully the girls are at an age where they can finally pitch in. But sometimes the dishes don't all get washed right away. Sometimes the bedtime story may be a bit abbreviated because Mommy or Daddy is tired and needs to go "night, night" too. And sometimes it means that it's 12:44 a.m., I am not sleepy at all, but rather I am awake, putting a few thoughts down on paper to share, so that someone like you can read them.

Beware of Hand-Me-Downs

Beware of hand-me-downs. That's all I have to say. They seem harmless on the surface, helpful actually, and money-saving. But after spending an hour this morning sifting through a drawer jam-packed with clothes, many that were well-loved and somewhat stained with graphics tattered after too much laundering (having arrived already worn), I've concluded that hand-me-downs are not the cost-free gifts they appear to be.

It starts innocently enough. Beautiful, almost never worn tiny clothes that are truly a joy to receive and see worn on one's little ones. But this short infant phase is suddenly followed by hand-me-downs that are more than slightly used, their former owners' young children who evidently trampled in the mud or played in the dirt. These items, while

132 Balancing Three

new to us, were already clearly well used and enjoyed.

But the pattern has stuck, the girls delight at the new arrivals and are already arguing over who gets what. The clothing that was recently purchased with love by their mother gets pushed to the back of the drawer in favor of the items that they've selected from the newly-presented pile of hand-me-downs.

There's absolutely no room to store it all. I consider the options. The one that seems the most logical, at this moment anyway, is to tell our friends that while we appreciate their generosity and good intentions, our closets are out of space.

The few dollars saved? Not meaningful enough when you factor in the time spent and lost rummaging through a cluttered closet, cluttered drawers, and the impact of the overall lack of organization on the whole proces of getting three girls ready for school in the morning.

Will anyone's feelings be hurt? I don't think so. Will the girls miss the hand-me-down arrival "shopping spree?" Probably not. I try to absorb this likely new gift receiving policy, knowing it will be a good one, for the time being, at least.

As I survey the artwork that surrounds me on desk, piano

bench and loveseat—stacks of it—I sigh, for this is yet another challenge to tackle regarding what to keep and what not. Lacking a solution for the moment, I vow to solve this problem another day.

Less is More

Three car seats. Three swings. Three cribs, then toddler beds, followed by three tricycles, three scooters, roller blades and bicycles. Three sets of homework and art projects, and three of every type of clothes to wear. The cuteness is overwhelming, and so is the sheer volume of everything that needs to find a place to go.

I'm touching upon an area in which I admittedly have a weakness. I shared my story about the childhood closet jammed to the hinges whose contents cascaded onto the floor when my unsuspecting father went looking for something or another…

After nearly nine years of parenthood, I still haven't come up with a system that works for me. Binders. That's my latest effort. Somebody please help me to actually file or toss. File or toss.

Habits begin early and apparently don't change without conscious intent, because I am still a victim of my own tendencies to jam the drawers and closets and then forget what I own, opting instead for the ease of leaving the necessities in sight and within quick reach, a habit that perhaps is not ideal with a neatnik husband and young triplet girls, in a relatively small house.

I raise this subject because I believe it bears addressing, this matter of keeping one's house in order while parenting triplets, or any child for that matter. I realize and notice now that my housekeeping habits are mirrored back to me by my own children.

Adopting my habits, my children view a stack of paper and arts and crafts supplies sitting on a countertop (along with other things) as normal, and don't feel the need to find a storage place for them any more than I do. For me personally, the matter has filtered into the subject of preserving my marriage, as my husband has repeatedly voiced his intolerance for any non-decorative items left "out," rather than easily stored somewhere in a drawer, or in a cabinet, out of view.

It's become no joking matter, my husband's harmony upset by what he considers offensive—namely, any stack of paper, of any kind, in view. He tries to tolerate my less-than-perfect storage methods, but every now and then his patience ebbs. This morning he offhandedly mentioned that clutter, so he'd heard, has now been documented as being a leading cause of depression in adults.

I admit, when confronted with my husband's intolerance for my less-than-perfect housekeeping habits (i.e., procrastination regarding filing or dealing with mail or other paper items, which tend to accumulate in a pile), I've over the years cycled between anger, resentment, self-pity and elbow grease. This last option is an actual attempt on my part to address the clear need for organization, or more precisely, the need to eliminate, discard, and keep fewer possessions.

My style, in my husband's perception, is devoid of any actual organization. His style, which is rigidly based upon everything having its place and everything being put promptly in its correct place, is perhaps a better model for our children to emulate. And so, I've made efforts and strides in bridging the gap between my ingrained habits and my husband's innate need for order. "Less is more," as they say.

This runs counter to my instincts, as I like to consider myself thrifty and resourceful. This causes me often to retain some things, thinking they may hold future use, when in fact we'd be better served to throw them away or donate them to others.

I have to remind myself that the household will be neater and cleaner by letting some things go, to create space and maintain an orderly surrounding, even if it means having to spend money down the line to replace them. I'm trying to train myself to dispose or donate whenever possible. There's just no room to act otherwise.

I know I'm sentimental. I love seeing artwork prepared by my girls, even artwork a year or two old. Recently I began decorating the walls of their rooms with their most promising drawings, as a means of reducing the pile of finished works from the tabletops and drawers. I've started to throw out (yes, I'm learning) some undeveloped sketches that I thought wouldn't be missed by the girls, and that also wouldn't cause me any regret in the fact of discarding them. Occasionally I've taken photos of some art works that

I thought I might enjoy seeing in photo form, as a means of preserving the memory, while still serving the purpose of eliminating the paper pile. I've enjoyed the end result of fewer stacks of miscellaneous papers that clutter, leaving more room for creativity and new projects.

This morning I spent some time rooting through a cupboard that had an odd assortment of goody bag contents: arts and crafts supplies, playing cards and paper. I contemplated the advice I recently read in a book on the subject of organization, suggesting one pretend to be a kindergarten teacher when organizing a cupboard full of random contents.

Perhaps with this virtual hat on, I'll be less haphazard with my cleanup, and more tidy with my organization. Maybe, just maybe, the end result will look more visually appealing, and be more functional for daily use. Note to self: don't let your cupboards get so jammed full that you can't tell what they contain.

The fact is, there's a neverending onslaught of child-related papers, toys, possessions and treasures, and it can pile up faster than you can say the words, "They're triplets. No, they are not identical."

And as they say, "whatever you do, your kids will mirror back at you."

Shopping

In the days before the girls were able to walk, I generally did my grocery shopping alone. The triplet stroller I had selected with its 45-pound frame wasn't exactly the easiest to pull in and out of the rear of first my Honda Pilot, and then my Honda Odyssey minivan. While it may have been convenient for traversing doorways and narrow sidewalks, it was not as ideal for short trips to the store, requiring, if not a human helper, at least a nearby curb with which to prop the device so it wouldn't roll off into the distance, or worse yet, into oncoming traffic. Someone had forgotten, or elected against, the idea of a wheel stop. Oops.

The unloading and propping of our empty stroller required first unfolding it without pinching one's fingers in the metal joints, so that the open frame would then be ready to accept its small passengers. When the girls were still in infant carrier seats, these snapped easily into place in the frame. But the loading and unloading process itself took time, and crowded parking lots didn't feel like the safest place to take on the challenge of loading three little ones, one at a time. So with the logistics of three infants in carriers, as you might imagine, the girls rarely accompanied me to the store.

When the girls could finally walk, I braved the supermarket with them. What an adventure! I'd grab my essentials–keys, purse, phone, and empty shopping bags—and we'd nervously make our way across the parking lot (well, I was nervous, anyway).

"Hold hands!" I'd direct the third in line, having only two hands to offer them myself. I was all eyes and ears and somewhat reminiscent of Popeye in the cartoon episode in which he's learning to drive, his head swiveling around 180 degrees to see in all directions at once. That about sums it up.

When we've finally made it to the front door (hoorah for me!), then there's another scenario that has happened more than once.

"Let's get that cart!" Lily shouts, pointing to the cart that has a toy red car attached. The car/cart combo was probably about seven feet in length, yielding a new dilemma. There was only room in the toy car for two children.

"I'll take that one!" Everest yells back, pointing to a second cart, this one with a toy blue car attached.

I look at Lily and Mia sitting in the first little red car, excitedly waiting for me to push them along into the store and between the aisles of fully stocked grocery shelves. Everest has already hopped into the blue car, happily oblivious to my challenge.

"I can only push one cart, Everest. Please climb into the child seat on this one," I soothe, as the corners of her mouth turn down.

"But I want to ride in the blue car!" she cries.

"We'll take turns," I try again, willing my voice to calm her. "Lily and Mia, Everest will get her turn in a few minutes, and one of you will sit in my shopping cart."

I reason with them, all the while knowing that the moment of transfer will bring new tears and a likely lack of cooperation. And so it goes.

On the days when the grocery store doesn't happen to have any carts available with toy cars attached, the new seat of choice is the child seat next to the cart's handlebars. One child will always be first to request that seat, followed nearly in unison by the other two, "I want that seat! I want that seat!"

The "unlucky" two satisfy themselves by hopping over the side and into the cart itself, which then results in the logistical challenge of finding room to place the actual groceries, which were the objective of the shopping expedition in the first place. I may have surreptitiously placed one or two smashed loaves of white bread back on the shelves in favor of unbruised merchandise during these adventurous outings. Shhh, don't tell Vons.

As the girls became more active, sitting in the cart was replaced by one girl hopping on the lower rack of the cart with her feet, hanging onto the side of the cart with her hands, balanced by a second sister on the other side of the cart doing exactly the same, with the third sister hanging onto the end, facing me while I pushed the now nearly 100 pound load.

I am then necessarily at the ready, steeling myself and anticipating the likelihood of one child jumping off the cart suddenly to exclaim and point, "Ooh, buy this!"—which would alter the precarious balance of my load of now only two children rather than three, with less than sufficient weight on one side to hold the contraption on solid ground unless the child on the opposite side thinks (or is asked politely "Get off") to hop off as well.

The appeal of the child seat seems to be waning these days; apparently it's much more interesting to be able to point at the shelves from a standing position in order to shout, "Can we buy this?" "What about that?" and race off down the aisle in search of other tempting purchase options to propose, or to throw in the cart on the sly.

I am routinely bombarded with rapid-fire requests "Ooh! I want this!" and more recently "I'll pay for it!" (using chore money), small fingers reaching excitedly for colorful merchandise, food or snacks, eyes dancing, requiring Momma to make split-second practical choices.

"OK. No, not that. Put that back. Watch out for that lady!"

At times, the girls have wandered off, leaving me calling "Everest! Mia, stay here!" And then "Lily, do you know where Everest went?!"

And I have on past occasions, with mounting panic, shouted, "Everest! Where are you?" as I raced up one aisle and down the next in order to reconnect with my young child lest my worst fears be realized (you never know if there's an ill-intentioned adult lurking, taking advantage of the less-than-perfect supervision, ready to pounce and kidnap your child).

There's my quest for perfection again. It's just not possible. These days I've reverted to doing much of my shopping alone, the relative peace and serenity of which allows me to complete the errand in a more reasonable period of time, rather than the extended visit resulting from three ponytailed girls running up and down the aisles in various directions. Solo outings also yield calm and unhurried purchase decisions, I reason, unpressured by three inquiring young minds interjecting their spontaneous desires upon me for consideration, testing my boundaries and learning their (and my) limits. So for now, anyway, it's generally me and the cart and the open aisle.

What's it like, you ask, raising triplets? Sometimes you just need to leave them behind, and take a moment to catch your breath alone.

Managing Three

I have to say, I couldn't manage this business of parenting three very well without my husband. We volley the ball back and forth with whatever needs doing. Whether it's breakfast prep or driving-to-school duty, Simon's on deck. But as their mom, I would say without stretching the truth too much, that I manage, by and large, everything else relating to the girls' care. It's what I would call the traditional, perhaps even now outdated model, of the husband bringing home the bacon, and the wife managing the household. It's sometimes a heavy load. But I've grown accustomed to its rigor, and my repayment is the love I get from them all. And I've managed to reduce my work commitments, working smarter, and fewer, hours, so that I can be a stay-at-home mom during at least the afternoon portion of my day. The division of labor is a constant work in progress, I have to admit. Tonight we had a family dinner together, and Simon cleaned up the kitchen after we finished eating. I took time for myself (writing this) while he read to the girls, first Mia and Everest in their room, and then Lily in hers. Although Simon generally favors scratching the girls' backs over reading as his nighttime act of parental love. I'm the reader in the family. Simon jokes that he would read a book, if he only knew how. It's all in fun; he most certainly knows how to read, and he has an extensive vocabulary to boot.

Simon has made it a practice, whenever the occasion permits, to take the girls out individually, so that both he and the lucky selected girl can experience some "Daddy and me" time. It's not as often as he'd like (he's got his own workload to manage) but every so often Simon will take one girl with him, maybe even away for an overnight outing to the desert, a favorite destination of his, or sometimes on a mundane errand to the hardware store. He seems to love this one-on-one time, and I always envy him that he's taken this initiative, but I seldom do the same. I'm too much of a softy; I hate leaving anyone behind. I wouldn't want to be the one left out, myself. This probably harks back to my middle school days; I had too many childhood experiences of getting left out of "the group"...and now I do my best to include everyone, all the time, as much as possible. But Simon fits in his weekend one-on-one times with his girls, rotating first one, then the next, and they have grown accustomed to the pattern, knowing that their turn will come, if not that day, then another. Often the lucky girl will come home with a new stuffed animal, their dad's way of rewarding them for their time alone with him. I don't begrudge him the small expense. Whatever works, I figure. And if the outing is just to the hardware store, a reward for that particular excursion might well be in order.

The girls and I go most places as a unit. I've eliminated from my repertoire quite a few activities that I found exhausting, or those that presented too many point-of-purchase temptations.

One little requested item, such as "Mommy, can I have that bear?" can suddenly turn into a $30, $40 or even $50 purchase when multiplied by three, and a more robust $30 item times three entails a $100 expenditure, which I don't necessarily make just because of three young hopeful faces pointed in my direction. I sometimes wonder how all the larger families out there do it. Taking a family of five, even out to eat, is simply costly.

And so we avoid some places that others may go to routinely, such as Disneyland, for instance. Last year Simon made a valiant attempt to manage all three when taking the girls to a father-daughter dance. How does *that* work you might wonder? Not very well, I'm afraid. All three girls wanted to dance with Daddy at the same time. Dancing in a circle was the solution, if I recall correctly. Even mundane matters such as crossing the street, or traversing a busy parking lot, as heretofore described, require nerves of steel and hyper-vigilance. Today, the girls and I spent the morning together at Sunday school. It was the first day of a new school, so I chose to reinforce my support for the activity by being either in the room or nearby. We headed afterward to visit a friend with three kids of similar ages for a quick play date. Thankfully, my time with the mom was as rewarding as the kids' time with their friends seemed to be—a fairly rare, but definitely welcome occurrence.

Yesterday morning I spent a few minutes on the floor with Lily, engaging in a game of pretend play with her dolls. Today, I sang a song with Everest that she had learned in

Sunday school, and was trying to teach to me. And Mia and I had a chat while she was in the bath, then while I combed her hair, and while she flossed her teeth...exchanges of words that I hoped would be teaching moments for her, but were also a time for me to communicate, to show care, and to simply be her mom.

I find that I also rotate my attentions, in a manner of speaking, measuring as I go so as not to leave any one girl left wanting, careful to validate the girls as their own individuals. I'm ever sensitive to their perception that I'm granting equal attention, which lurks in the background each and every moment, and affects the decisions that I make each and every day. Sometimes I choose clockwise, another day counter clockwise—"pick me," "pick me," not always spoken, but the undercurrent is there, ready to rebuke me should I ever fail to offer equal attention, equal provisions, or equal anything at all.

I do my best to affirm the differences between my girls as well as to honor their individual preferences. I want them to know, and to also feel, that I see them as unique, and as a group only in the aspect that they are all my daughters.

So when people ask, wondering about my experience

mothering triplets, "How *do* you do it"? I'm somewhat at a loss for an appropriate answer.

I shrug more often than not, lacking a ready and pithy reply. I might say upon reflection, "With a little help from my friends."

And I don't know anything different, happily. So, when people remark "Triplets? What's that like?"

I can answer, and mean it…"It's fun. Good times."

Most of the time, anyway.

Sleepovers

"You're invited to a sleepover," I happily confided to Lily. "Don't tell your sisters until after I tell them. I don't want them to be upset."

"Really?! I am?" Lily responded excitedly. "Where??"

"At Josefina's. Just you."

I'd been wondering when the girls might have the opportunity to experience a "sleepover" play date for some months now. I'd overheard conversations amongst a few of the kids at school, and it seemed that some of them had been enjoying such overnight adventures. With three kids the same age, I'd made a mental note that my girls might not be first on the invite list for sleepovers. Who would have the room, much less the energy, to host three girls for a night?

And now this mom, a friend of mine, unabashedly invited

just Lily, knowing that her daughter had bonded with Lily in particular on their most recent play date. This had inadvertently solved the dilemma.

"Everest. Mia. I have something to tell you and I don't want you to be upset. Lily's been invited to a sleepover, by herself, at Josefina's. Her mom can't invite all of you. Eventually you'll have a sleepover too. Someone will invite you to go by yourself for a sleepover."

Everest's round brown eyes began to fill with tears as she contemplated the great fortune her sister Lily had just encountered, the mysterious and desirable sleepover play date invitation. Mia announced, worriedly, "But I don't want to go by myself!"

This outburst seemed to calm Everest down, who now busied herself with soothing her sister. Everest turned toward Mia, quickly drying her own eyes. "But our turn will be next," she said softly to Mia. "We can go together."

I didn't correct the explanation, figuring time would tell how the actual circumstance would unfold. Lily was practically jumping in her seat in anticipation during the fifteen-minute ride home from school.

When we arrived home, Lily busied herself in her room.

"I'm packed!" she announced, coming out no more than five minutes later. I entered her room to investigate. In a backpack, Lily had placed toothbrush, toothpaste, nightgown, and a change of clothes. On top of the backpack rested her small baby blanket and a book to read. At the time she was not yet even seven years old...this kid was unbelievable.

An hour later, the four of us were in the car, driving Lily over to her play date. Everest and Mia had come along for the ride, and to wish their sister well. I looked at Lily's young face in the car's rear view mirror. Her gap-toothed smile was uncontrollably ear-to-ear. When we arrived at our destination a few short minutes later, Lily climbed out of the car and up the front stairs of her friend's house.

"Have fun!" we chorused. "See you tomorrow."

Lily raised her hand in a wave, giving us a big brave smile, and eventually turned to begin her adventure alone, blankie, book and backpack in hand.

A Few House Rules

After finding myself repeatedly picking up after my kids, handling tasks that they've grown old enough to handle on their own, I decided about a year ago to establish some house rules. These were met with some degree of enthusiasm and vigor when first announced, although I have to admit that my rigor in enforcing them has been less than perfect.

I do recommend house rules. Of course, they probably work better if the parent enforces them. I know from my own childhood experience that some parents, especially us moms, maintain the habit of cleaning up after their kids long after we should. This is not only unhelpful to our children in the long-run, it is tiresome and also time consuming for us. We're left with less time and freedom to enjoy our day and more stress and strain to absorb. With a little bit of training, and positive reinforcement, kids can be taught to do the basics, leaving only the most adult of clean-up tasks to the older generation.

So I'll share my original list of house rules with you. Feel free to copy, modify, or make your own.

1. Give Mommy and Daddy kisses and hugs every day.
2. Listen to whoever is in charge (Mommy, Daddy, or babysitter) when we say something (the first time!)
3. If you want to visit your friends down the block you must discuss it with Mommy, Daddy or babysitter to get permission before leaving the house.
4. Wash your hands and mouth after eating (we haven't quite gotten into the rigor of daytime tooth brushing… there's always next year).
5. Leave the room the way you found it! This means: (a.) Clean up and put away all paper, art supplies, and dishes. (b.) Find a place to store or hang the artwork you love. (c.) Find a place to store the school work you'd like to keep (storage boxes under your beds is one suggestion).
6. Put your shoes in your shoeboxes when you take them

off. Do NOT leave them in the living room, kitchen, or any room you happen to be in at the time. (I've realized that I am the worst offender in the house with regard to this particular rule.)
7. Put all dirty clothes in the hamper (not on the floor).
8. Don't put anything on Mommy's desk.
9. Don't put anything on the couch behind Mommy's desk.
10. Don't put anything on the piano bench.
11. Put caps on all markers and put them away when finished.
12. Help with meal preparation or setting the table.
13. Help with after meal clean up.
14. Bring your plate to the sink after you've finished your meal or snack.
15. Dry your feet before you leave the bathroom.
16. Hang up your bath towel after drying off (don't leave it on the floor).
17. Dry your feet after being in the pool, before you enter the house.
18. No ball playing in the house.
19. No throwing of anything (including pillows) in the

house.

20. No feet on any furniture (beds, sofas, et cetera) unless you are lying down.
21. Knock before opening a closed door.
22. If you walk through a closed door, close it again after you walk through it.
23. When you enter the house, take off your shoes if they are dirty or wet.
24. Mommy or Daddy may add to this list from time to time.
25. Children's suggestions for this list may also be considered, if Mommy and Daddy agree with them.

Note to parent: I suggest you post your list somewhere at kids' eye level, or it may get lost or stuck under a stack of artwork. Don't ask me how I know this.

Too Much TV

"The garbage man is here," I call, vainly trying to distract the girls from their latest obsession, watching Netflix programs for kids on their Chrome computers, a well-intentioned but bad-result gift from their grandpa this past December.

Nobody moves from the screen. I don't think I hear even a "wha?" or grunt of any kind, so affixed they are to the story unfolding in animation before their eyes. It used to be that the girls lined up in front of the bay window at the front of our house, fascinated by the operation of the mechanical arm that surrounded the trash and recycle cans, lifting them up, dumping their contents and then placing them back next to the sidewalk before moving along to the next house.

I used to feel a neighborly camaraderie with the

garbage man, who most likely was very pleased with the unaccustomed attention provided by the girls to his weekly task. He routinely honked at the girls and waved, delighting them with his acknowledgement of their presence.

This morning I went out on my own to pick up the newspaper on the driveway, another task that the girls fought over only a few short years ago, but have now abandoned (been there, done that).

I wave at the garbage man, he waves back, both of us likely feeling wistful that the children of the household no longer find this occasion noteworthy, having moved on to manmade screen dramas and other more apparently magnetic attractions.

I linger on the porch and continue to watch the truck's motions as the metal arm encircles, lifts and empties first one can and then the next. I feel oddly rooted to the ground until the truck finally groans its movement along the street to service our next door neighbor's house.

I vow to reconsider the household policy regarding screen time, which I know will be a losing and quite unpopular proposition, and then open the paper to my favorite page, the horoscope. Some mindless pleasures endure.

Less is More Part II

Following a childhood sometimes passed in pursuit of my father's approval, I seem so far destined to live a life in search of that elusive two percent that would allow me to give myself a perfect 100% score. But in my experience, many moments are lost, and goals are sometimes dismissed as unattainable when seeking perfection. I don't recommend it.

Now, *mon grand fait accompli*, having triplets, has given me the opportunity to experience the ultimate test of doing everything "just right." It's funny, I didn't realize until just recently how much my drive for perfection affects my nearly every move and decision. And it will always be a losing battle. I try to remind myself that this is what it means to be human...we are not perfect beings.

In my quest to be the perfect mom, I've done my best to expose my girls to as many new activities as I could physically manage to arrange. In the beginning, the girls were interested in just about everything. But after a few years now of dealing with the mechanics of getting them to and from—with appropriate attire and snacks in hand—staying home has held larger and larger appeal...ironically to all of us.

Here is a list of what we've tried so far:

1. Playing musical instruments (piano mostly, this currently on hiatus, as no one wishes to practice)
2. Ballet dancing (didn't captivate)
3. Making art (remains a favorite)
4. Baking (we all love)
5. Learning gymnastics (also still a favorite)
6. Golfing
7. Swimming
8. Water skiing
9. Ice skating
10. Horseback riding
11. Snow skiing

12. Sledding
13. Rollerblading
14. Roller skating
15. Zip lining
16. TV and film auditions and filming
17. Hula Hooping
18. Playing Bocci ball
19. Reading books
20. Doing jigsaw puzzles

And this list does not include what would seem these days to be mandatory: outings to Disneyland, Legoland, the LA and San Diego zoos, the library, local parks and the beach. Or the two most definitely non-obligatory sightseeing trips we took with the girls to France.

What's left? I'm sure there's more, but at the moment only tennis and martial arts come to mind. At the tender age of eight, I can only think of those two activities that I haven't yet exposed my girls to in any fashion, and these will soon be added to the list of "tried that" activities too, no doubt.

I think this is more and more common, albeit not necessarily desirable, this quest to have one's child try each and every imaginable activity as soon as possible after being able to walk and talk. In our case, the girls have begun to dismiss one activity after the next, opting instead for the familiarity and comfort of staying home and playing in the backyard (or of course, watching their beloved Chrome books).

We've encouraged the girls to participate in the same activities, because practically speaking, are we really going to drive three separate places in one afternoon just to engage in a little fun extra-curricular time? We've been whittling down our list, and giving higher priority to those activities that promote family togetherness.

I took a golf lesson with Everest and Lily last spring, for instance, while Mia went off to the homework club. I had asked all the girls in turn if they were interested in continuing to learn golf. Lily and Everest gave me an enthusiastic "yes!" while Mia responded, "uh...not so much" (I'm not even paraphrasing. The line is fine between an eight year old and their future teenage self). So there's one instance of splitting up the troops that may happen more and more as time goes on. And I'm sure we'll stick with the tried and true fallback of art time at home, an easily-managed activity that seems to suit all our energy levels (mine included). Perhaps we'll get back to piano one of these days.

So, what's it like, you might still ask, to raise triplets?

1. There is no shortage of joy. Wherever you look there is a small face to greet you, and thankfully we are still in the stage where the face is generally anxious to please.
2. There is an overabundance of artwork, lovingly created, generally as gifts and also as an exploration ("blue plus yellow makes green").
3. There is a never-ending opportunity, as a parent, to be a better person, and to learn to control one's emotions, reactions and verbal outpourings.

When I think of what it means to me, to be the perfect mom, I picture baking cookies and doing art. I see beach outings with a picnic lunch, and making sand castles with moats and princesses. I think of bike rides exploring new destinations, and singing and dancing to music. This is all doable.

Now for the two percent part, my take on the characteristics of a perfect mom's household (which apparently is not so doable for me):

1. Their children's closets are perfectly organized, as are their own.
2. Their house is immaculate with artwork and family photos beautifully displayed on cute boards in designated areas of the home, and the rest safely closeted away (or the unthinkable, thrown away).
3. Dinner is on the table flawlessly at 6:00 p.m. sharp, and children are bathed, hair combed and dressed in pajamas already.
4. Ragged clothing is tossed in the trash, along with the several-days-old dinner leftovers, without regret, and with appreciation for it having given so much pleasure or sustenance.
5. Fresh flowers are placed in pleasing vases on select table tops where appropriate (OK, this last may be more about being the perfect housewife, but flowers give everyone pleasure, so I thought I'd throw it in.)

Things perfect moms don't do:

1. They don't yell at their children.
2. We won't even discuss taboo physical punishment such as spanking etc., when children are misbehaving. THAT is something perfect moms DEFINITELY don't do.
3. They don't brush their children's hair too vigorously when they are in a rush or mad about not having enough help with the kids or around the house.
4. They don't just "get through" any planned event. Perfect moms enjoy each and every moment, and are relaxed when hosting, wisely hiring help for setup and cleanup so that they can actually converse with their friends and guests.

I think this last one bears elaboration. I have found myself overwhelmed by so much "doing" that at times I haven't enjoyed the destination that took so much effort to get to. So in my wiser, ninth year of motherhood, I can now suggest to any expectant or current mom, with a reasonable amount of firsthand experience to back it up, that the adage "less is more" has merit, and should be considered in place of an overabundance of trips and experiences.

I've realized that being mentally present for a moment when my daughter's eyes light up at something new, requires not feeling harried because I forgot to bring an extra pair of socks, or a jacket, or a snack, or whatever else happens to be missing in a moment of need. If you're like me, you'll find it's quite easy to get in the habit of berating yourself for the one thing you forgot, and in the process of feeling that regret, miss the enjoyment of what you came there to share and experience anew, through your child's eyes.

So I'd now suggest, after years of not following this advice; when in doubt, opt for less than perfection—or better yet, come up with your own definition of what 'perfect' means in your life. For me, it's one activity less, and one hug more. Just a moment on the steps, gazing out at the birds, or flowers, or other children playing. Feet in the grass, little hands in mine, with nothing pressing to do, this is what it means to me, to be the perfect mom.

A Mother's Love

"We've been traveling so much I don't know where home is anymore. I guess it's here." My mom smiled at me.

We were lying side by side on her bed, her frequent resting position after a non-grueling morning of getting up and eating her breakfast. My mom is 88 and has been struggling with the simple act of breathing for a few years now. Her lungs just don't seem to work well any longer, the belated and undesirable result of a long ago bout with pneumonia.

"Home is where the heart is, right?" I respond.

Mom gets up for something and comes back into the bedroom and lays down again.

"We've been traveling so much. I don't know where home is anymore," she repeats with a smile. "I guess it's here."

Mom's memory had been misfiring in the last year. She

often repeats things she says during the same conversation, not remembering that she already shared a particular story or anecdote. I smile back at her, and repeat my response, guessing that she did not recall we had just had this short exchange. "Home is where the heart is, right?"

My mom is the perfect antidote to my dad's strong and unyielding influence. She is and has been an angel to put up with my dad's varying moods, and is forever sweet, gentle, generous and giving. I admired and wished to emulate my dad as a young twentysomething and thirtysomething, working hard to succeed in my chosen career. And while my mom always remained a constant loving presence, she didn't provide the career role model I sought, as she elected to work alongside my dad as his assistant during my adolescent years. I saw myself as the main event in my own career, and her role of being on the sidelines to my dad's career didn't stimulate my young ambitions.

As a mom now myself, working from home, balancing the needs of three young children, my husband, our household and our business (oh right, and my needs too, lest I forget!), I see now that the role model my mom offered me was most perfect. After all, what is more impactful than a mother's love?

When I was in kindergarten, my mom stormed over to have a word with the mom of a little boy who bullied me and who tore up my lovingly created drawing of a house. When I was in middle school my mom bought me a beautiful long winter coat, just because I mentioned another schoolmate had a new coat that I admired. When I was in high school, my mom drove me to a fundraising walkathon, willing to support me in whatever activity my young mind wished to pursue. And my mom made each and every payment on my four years of college loans, happily informing me ten years later, "It's all paid off."

I was mortified, somehow not realizing that the cost had been financed, and feeling regret on her behalf. I also questioned the value of my college education.

"Was it worth it?" I asked her, feeling somehow guilty about the extent and duration of her investment.

"Oh yes!" she responded sincerely. It didn't make me feel any better somehow.

Now that my mom is in her sunset years, in the plural we hope, I cherish her soft-spoken ways and wish at times that I could be more like her. It's ironic how things I valued before having children seem to hold less meaning for me now. Sitting with one of my daughters, and really listening to what she has to say, is more important to me now than any business deal, or other action I might take. And for this, my mom was, and still is, the most perfect example.

It's that Time of Year Again

Halloween has just passed. I'm already feeling the tug of momentum of energy that leads us to the end of the year with all the joys and related stresses and strains it brings. For Momma, that is. I made my annual visit to the garage to pull out last year's box of decorations, noting which had survived the year of storage, and which might be better suited for the donation box or trash bin.

This year, the girls wore their Halloween costumes three times, leaving them a little bedraggled looking by the time we got to the main event. The costumes looked their finest for an early Halloween party held at Chuck E. Cheese by a family friend. They still looked reasonably fresh for their second wearing during the school's Halloween parade. And then came the day of Halloween itself, one that the girls had looked forward to with so much excited anticipation.

"How many days until Halloween, Momma?" they asked me, one after the other, day after day. "Not counting today, and not counting Halloween," they asked again, wanting it to be sooner, rather than later, not using the traditional method of counting, but their own unique technique.

Before the girls were old enough to pick their own costumes, we dressed them alike for Halloween, unlike the other days of the year. Their first year of real trick-or-treating, when they were just under three years old, they were adorably outfitted as hula dancers, with green grass skirts and coconut shells like a bikini top over pale pink leotards. The following year they wore pastel colored, high-collared Chinese pajamas with matching parasols. That particular accessory turned out to be highly impractical during the actual trick-or-treating, challenging their dexterity by taxing both hands with things to carry. In the two years that followed, the girls had their own ideas of which costume they'd like to wear. In the first year they all dressed similarly, even given the choice to themselves, as princesses. In the second year, we had two superhero girls (Lily and Mia) and one zebra (Everest, my animal lover), as the girls chose their outfits based upon their own developing individual preferences.

This year Everest and Mia dressed alike as a flying dog character named "Sky" from the TV show *Paw Patrol*, an animated series that the middle-aged and older homeowners handing out candy didn't quite recognize (me in that category as well). Lily dressed as a zebra princess, replete with crown. She looked less "in costume" and more or less as she herself would be dressed on any given day, apt as she is to stylishly combine prints and patterns. That evening, while sorting through her full basket of treats, she stated to the rest us matter-of-factly, "I'm not going to be twins with anyone next year either," asserting her intentions of individuality for that future date.

That's my girl. If you'd like a clearer visual for the little Miss Lily, Google "Fearless Girl" on msn.com. The bronze statue is currently installed on Wall Street in Manhattan. It looks startlingly like her.

It's now a week later, and the three candy baskets are still nearly full. We regulate the girls' candy consumption by requiring the earlier intake of some protein or another—at a minimum that being a glass of chocolate milk. The girls appear happy and content, knowing that there are more celebrations ahead.

"Which holiday is next? Everest asked yesterday, ready to happily begin her anticipation. "Is it Christmas?"

"No, Thanksgiving is next," I answered, with a smile.

Oh, to be a child.

Birthdays and the Holidays

I pull out my virtual surfboard to ride our end of year tidal wave. The girls' birthday is on December 12th, which is typically followed by Chanukah. The highlight of the last month of the year remains, birthdays aside, undeniably Christmas.

We established an early custom of singing happy birthday to each girl individually, with a special and individual birthday cake for each child, to provide her with her own special moment. After all, she was already sharing her special day. So for the first three birthday celebrations, we sang happy birthday three times. The girls then began attending a French immersion language school, and at that school we got in the habit of singing happy birthday in multiple languages. And since then each year we've sung happy birthday nine times. Of course we needed to sing in English and French; Spanish somehow got thrown into the mix as well.

The girls have seemed satisfied, so far any way, with the song and cake being the few select shining moments for themselves alone, apparently willing to share the spotlight during the party itself. This year may be the year that we break that tradition.

Chanukah is next, which we celebrate by playing with dreidels and eating gold foil-wrapped chocolate "coins." With Christmas not far off, we long ago decided to eliminate gifts from our Chanukah celebration. Enough is enough.

Although I was raised Jewish, and still consider myself as such, it was, as a child, not the most happy selection of religion, leaving me as it did outside the fanfare and fuss of Christmas fever, which even then infused many activities, in school or otherwise. I remember feeling left out of the celebration, which caused my parents to try and console me by erecting a dead tree from our yard in our living room, and referring to it as a Chanukah bush. It looked odd and not especially festive, and somehow didn't fill the gap left by our not celebrating the birth of Jesus, which seemed to me was celebrated by the entire rest of the world. Well, if not the whole world, then at least everyone excepting the families that attended our local synagogue. So G-d please forgive me, but I always secretly wished I could celebrate, too.

I finally got my wish, marrying "outside the faith" as they say. Simon isn't religious. He loves Easter and Christmas, and his celebrations of those holidays center largely around the fictional characters created for children's unique enjoyment, those of the Easter Bunny and Santa Claus. After we met, I happily joined Simon in celebrating first Christmas, then Easter, and purchasing chocolate or decorations and gifts, as the occasions warranted. It wasn't until the girls were born that suddenly these fun-filled holidays took on an aspect of responsibility and added to my already full agenda.

Despite our "no Chanukah gifts" decision, December is a month full of presents. Some are mailed in by relatives from out of state for the girls' birthday, or Christmas, or both. There's a continuous and seemingly never-ending influx of gifts for them to open. I'm sympathetic to all our friends and family who give the girls each a gift (that makes three) on their birthday, and generally also each a gift for Christmas too. And our close friends and relatives often make the effort to buy three unique, yet related gifts. Stripes for one, polka dots for another, and some other pattern for the third. Don't forget the favorite colors: now pink, light green and blue. Or three different crafts…the creativity with gift giving delights both the girls and me.

Since I didn't grow up with Christmas myself, I had no preconceived visions of the appropriate number of Christmas presents for a child to receive. When my husband suggested we not go crazy, given that the birthday presents were often not yet all unwrapped by the time Christmas rolled around, I didn't disagree. So, three presents each, for three young girls…our lives are a balance of threes, indeed.

Monday Mornings

Everest was my third born and the middle in birth weight at 4 lbs. 13 oz. Now she's the tallest by at least an inch, and because of that fact is often mistaken for being the "eldest." Everest has the heartiest and most diverse appetite of the three girls, often asking for second and third helpings when her sisters have long since finished their meal and are waiting for dessert.

Mia, born the heaviest and longest by an inch and an ounce, has over time dropped into middle position, so to speak. She seems to have gained weight by the forces of nature, rather than by eating good food. She just won't eat if the food doesn't pass her critical "looks good, smells good and presents well" test. I sometimes think she's trying to live on strawberries and chocolate milk alone. Lily is generally willing to try new foods, and eats enough protein I think, but has maintained her "runt of the litter" designation—she still stands an inch smaller and a pound less than Mia, this ranking having persisted for years now as the girls all grow.

I cater to the girls' individual food preferences, maybe to a fault. A new babysitter commented on this as I pulled down pasta and easy prep mac 'n' cheese from the shelf for her to prepare, "Oh. They don't eat the same thing?"

"No, I don't insist on it," I shrug and smile in response.

To me it's better to have all three girls consuming food, period, even if it results in a little more work for whoever is preparing the meal that particular day.

Most mornings I'm the family's de facto short order cook. "Good morning," I announce as I open the door to the girls' room.

It is 7:00 a.m. on Monday, time to be getting up and getting ready. The girls are awake, but still lying in their beds, cozy underneath their Ziggy sacks, a flannel blanket that hugs the twin mattress like a sheet, a Christmas present from last year. I lean down for morning kisses, "Rise and shine."

The California sun is already streaming through their

windows. Yet another sunny day here. I open the drapes to let in the sunshine, hoping this will help the girls rouse themselves.

"What do you want for breakfast?" I ask, already in motion down the hall toward the kitchen.

"Buttered raisin bread," Everest answers.

"I want French toast," I hear Lily's little voice call.

Mia doesn't answer, groggy as usual and perhaps waiting to hear me voice the request for her meal order two or three times before asking for a donut or a buttered baguette, or something else sweet. I accompany the sweet with chocolate milk, my rationale being that there's at least a little protein in the mix.

My movements are intentionally swift and efficient; I reach first to put bread in the toaster, rotating to open the fridge to retrieve the milk carton to pour Everest some milk. Eggs, bowl, cinnamon, coconut oil, pan, bread. I gather my ingredients, trying to remember to breathe as I work. I place the buttered raisin bread on the table in front of Everest and turn back around to the counter to dip the uncooked bread into the egg for Lily, adding a little cinnamon before using my spatula to put it into the now hot pan.

"I want butter on the French toast," Lily says to me.

"Say 'please,'" I intone, reminding her of her manners, handing her the butter and a knife. I cut the French toast while it's still cooking in the pan, and grab three napkins to place in front of my three now-seated breakfast patrons.

"Mia, what do you want?" I ask her for the second time.

"Frosted flakes," she mumbles, seating herself on the counter stool, still not quite awake.

I glance up at our kitchen clock, which now reads 7:20 a.m. Not bad. The girls are sitting, quietly eating, hair still disheveled, but mostly dressed. Still in socks, no shoes, I notice. I help myself to a cup of coffee from our new Keurig single-serve coffee machine, moving on from breakfast prep to filling water bottles for the girls to take with them to school. I throw a small snack into each girls' backpack. Apple for Everest, baguette for Mia, and tangerines for Lily. That'll work for today. We've long ago delegated the task of lunch preparation to the school cafeteria. Perhaps not the healthiest choice, but it makes my morning just a teensy bit easier.

Simon breezes into the kitchen, freshly showered and dressed. I've been up since 7:00 a.m., a reasonable hour by most people's standards. But I'm sweating with the urgency of all the aforementioned preparations, my heavy soft bathrobe long ago tossed aside. I'm in my skivvies now. What the heck, it's just family. Simon heads to the Keurig to prepare his own morning wake-up cup of coffee, and looks up to see the time. It's now 7:40 a.m.

"It's time to go!" he exclaims. "Get your shoes! Get your jackets! Get your backpacks!"

My heart jumps into my throat, an overreaction I know. The girls' plates are not yet empty. Mia is eating the frosted flakes with her fingers, ignoring the spoon I've provided. The girls all seem to prefer dry cereal, somehow. Call me a softy, I don't insist on the milk, I just encourage it.

"Wait, their hair is not brushed!" I wail, flustered at Simon's sudden announcement that it's time to go.

It always feels sudden, I realize, and premature in relation to our state of readiness. Simon pulls out the container of ponytail holders and hair clips from the cabinet and begins to brush Mia's hair. He's gotten quite good at it, I notice, surprised.

A few noisy minutes later Simon and the girls are all out the door, and the car is pulling out of the driveway, headed toward school. Quiet descends on me like a blanket. The spoils of breakfast are still on the table. I clean up quickly and sit down with my coffee cup at my computer to contemplate my day. I look out through our French doors into our green backyard, breathing deeply. The view greets me like an old friend.

What will the day bring? I take a deep breath once again, enjoying the feel of the empty house. It's my time now, I think, relishing the fact. For the next few hours, anyway.

Lily's Wants

I'm so tired right now. It's 3:45 p.m. on a Tuesday, and I'm ready for a nap. I'm actually not a napper, but it sounds like something that might be nice. I've noticed a pattern recently, which is that Lily has become the girls' and my activities director. I wasn't aware of the dynamic. Should've been, but it was subtle. And now I feel exhausted, ready to drop into bed, go horizontal, and just close my eyes. I often hear, "Triplets? You must be exhausted!" and today I feel it.

Actually, I often feel tired in the afternoon. But I'm not sure I can blame it solely on my triplets. It could be a hormonal imbalance, or the need for a more staggered caffeine intake. Or my low thyroid, or inconsistent sleep patterns? But I digress.

I've been dutifully administering the requests of our

little Miss Lily, and I realized this week that she's literally running my show. A few examples:

"Pick us up early from afterschool care. Please?!"

"Let's go to the Grove!" (The Grove is an outdoor L.A. shopping mall replete with a train trolley and candy and sticker stores.)

"I want to go to the park."

These exclamations are frequently expressed in her sweet, high octave, yet somewhat plaintive voice, accompanied by a slightly furrowed brow.

My quest to please, and my "I can do it if I try" brain kicks in. I contemplate the practicalities of fulfilling the request—logistics, timing, what else is on my agenda for the day, can my priorities be postponed? Etc., etc., etc.

Quite often Miss Lily gets her way, and her sisters are often pleased with the result, whether it's more time with Momma, or some other adventure. And all's good, except that I've let the control I felt I had over my own existence be usurped by an eight year old. And the end result at the present moment is that I'm stiff in the shoulders—a symptom of my stress level—and at the limit of my willingness to comply with the various and sundry demands of our little

Miss Lily. To make matters worse, last week I committed this afternoon to trying out a children's martial arts class, which none of the kids seem to be particularly enthused to attend, but are willing to try at my request.

Now it seems there are four of us who'd just as soon stay home and not go anywhere else this afternoon. I take a minute to reevaluate. Do we really need to go today? Maybe I can call and cancel. It's not exactly a time critical event. Happy with the idea, I pick up my phone to let the martial arts studio know. Tomorrow we will contemplate how to achieve a better balance between thee and me, but for now I'm going to enjoy a late afternoon cup of French Roast, and "take five" as they say.

The girls run outside to play in the yard, and I take a seat on our back deck to watch.

"This is good," I think to myself.

Martial arts will just have to wait.

Are they Identical? Part II

I knew early on that I didn't want to do the traditional thing by having my girls all dress alike. They already were three girls, as opposed to a mix of boys and girls, and de facto they were a unit "Triplets." So to me, dressing them alike was the equivalent of telling the world that they were all the same person. I avoided this almost like the plague, with a few exceptions for matching hats, or jackets. We might choose a dress or shirt of the same style, but generally in different colors. And by a very early age, we had established that Mia wore pink, Lily purple, and Everest yellow. To this day, Mia wears almost exclusively pink. Lily lately favors blue over purple, and Everest now favors lime green. It's funny how the girls each seem to choose a different color as their favorite.

Two of the girls have blue eyes, while Everest has brown, or hazel eyes. And while all the girls may be blonde, their locks are respectively and distinctively light (Lily), golden (Mia) and brownish-blond (Everest) to the discerning eye. Despite the dissimilarities, which to me are quite apparent, strangers, after asking, "Are they triplets?" will still exclaim, "Oh! Are they identical?"

"No, they're not identical," I smile in response. Isn't it obvious?! I'm thinking inside. The girls may be around the same in height, and they clearly came from the same gene pool, but they are definitely, positively, NOT identical.

Once you get to know them, you realize just how different they are. Nature vs. nurture I suppose. I have a natural born leader (Lily), who always wants to run the show, a most of the time willing follower, who is often referred to as timid, or shy (Mia), and my lovely peacemaker (Everest), who perfectly creates the balance between the three very different personalities who are my three precious and lovely daughters. And it's always been important to me that each of my girls' personalities shine. Because the reality is, I have three unique, individual and, luckily, loving daughters who just happen to have been born a minute apart.

192   Balancing Three

Mia is my "eldest" daughter. I say eldest simply as a means of differentiating. Mia is oldest by a minute. 8:01 a.m., as listed on her birth certificate (as compared to 8:02 and 8:03 a.m., the birth times of her two sisters). Mia doesn't behave as the eldest, but she dutifully raises her hand when people ask which girl is the oldest of the three, and by definition, she is.

When considering the dynamic between my three girls and me, it seems that Lily's strength in expressing her wishes has translated into those wishes often becoming fulfilled by a perhaps sometimes overly-obliging mother (me). Mia and Everest, both taller than my little Lily, are both generally more than happy to follow petite Lily's lead, until some other child enters the picture who is either older or more forceful, to impose his or her individual will on the dynamic of the seemingly compliant other two.

Lily hasn't learned yet how to deal with this circumstance, which often results in her being in tears and running to find me to air her distress. It's interesting to me how the combination of decisiveness and specificity of desire are expressed in Lily's leadership tendency, at least on home ground. With the less-decisive other two, it appears that their relative lack of prompt decision-making skills renders them willing to adopt (at least most of the time), the proposed games and play of their "leader by default" sister.

As time goes on, the girls' personalities continue to unfold. Lily in many ways is the most driven, being the quickest to embrace new activities that challenge her body and mind. She still also tends to be the most independent, although she recently moved back into the bedroom with her sisters, apparently missing their camaraderie. At the moment, Lily's hair is streaked with shades of pink, purple and blue, a temporary coloring treatment that we thought would do no harm, encouraging her individuality and sense of self.

Everest would heal the world, if she could. She is empathetic, considerate, and giving. And she continues to wear her emotions on her lovely and cute little face. Everest likes to help people, and her feelings are easily hurt if the object of her attention doesn't happen to want help, thank you. Everest is smart and interested in learning. She was our first reader of the three, reading with near fluency by the end of kindergarten—more than a year before Lily. Mia has just recently, at the age of eight, begun to read.

Mia's personality seems to shift depending upon her mood and confidence level. She's always been, and continues to be, an observer. She will watch and observe and then surprise you with her sudden confidence—driving a golf cart, for instance, or sledding down a snowy driveway on a winter trip to the mountains. Mia is also giving, quick to share with her sisters and her friends whatever treats I might buy, or to ask me if we can purchase a small gift to give to one of her sisters, or to another friend. Mia learns more slowly than her two sisters, and it's taken extra effort and tutoring to keep her from falling too far behind in school. This after-school task makes her grumpy and not at her best, but is one that she accepts, albeit grudgingly and with complaint. This latest new tutoring obligation requires a degree of time management on my part that sometimes results in me awarding less attention to the studies of the other two, who thankfully can manage without me in this regard, if need be. It's one more log in my load, this new chapter, that's for sure, but one that I carry with love and commitment.

The girls have their own built-in constant play date, including the "to be expected" typical sibling squabbles. But these are generally quickly resolved, though often with my involvement and gentle coaxing. There's a tremendous amount of love and caring that the girls all seem to have, one for the other.

I recently met a triplet dad who sadly lost one of his triplets at only four months old. It reminded me to be grateful for what we have, every single day. "Don't waste this one beautiful life," I read in a novel, not long ago. It unexpectedly moved me to tears. I wrote the words on a single sheet of white paper, using different colored markers for each word, and attached it with a magnet on our refrigerator, to act as a reminder to me to focus on appreciation, each and every day.

Three girls born on the same day, to the same parents, under the same set of stars above. Why should they be the same? G-d made us all unique creatures, and these three are no exception. I encourage their diversity and their individual style of dress. I encourage their sisterhood, but also their own unique skills as much as possible. They learn at different paces and sometimes have different interests. Eventually they will have different friends or even different circles of friends. They are sisters who happen to be the exact same age, and this is where the similarity ends.

"Are they identical?" you ask.

"Not at all," is my reply. "Take a closer look, and you will see."

The Balance between Three and Me

I realize that my daughters' entire short lives have led them to the conclusion that Momma is available to take care of their nearly every last need. Even now, tall enough and coordinated enough to help themselves to a glass of water on their own, or to pour lemonade from a container into a cup stored at a reachable height in the cabinet, they still regress to "I want" (this, or that), and tend to assume that I have nothing better to do than to help them fetch some item or another.

It's a tricky thing, finding that balance, between "them" and "me," in the equation of our relationship. Some days I take time for me, some days it's more about them. I try not to let too many days pass without doing something nice for either "one" of us. You might compare the give and take of it to a swing, which I found of interest to note is, in French, called a *balançoire*, meaning "to swing."

And that's what we do. Some for me, some for you. This way, and that. Back and forth, and so on.

As parents we are models for our children in so many things: our achievements, our willingness to express affection, our relationships with our spouses. It's so easy to get stuck or feel guilty about not always being physically available for them. It's also easy to lose sight of a more relevant facet of parenthood, namely demonstrating to our kids how to take care of their own needs, so that they in turn can become well-balanced and self-sufficient adults.

That requires setting boundaries, of course, and being self-preserving, which isn't always that easy to do. For me, much as I try to avoid taking on commitments that might overwhelm my already busy life, taking time for me is sometimes a pleasure I squeeze in, postpone, feel guilty about, or even forego when things get crazy or hectic.

When you're raising triplets, finding undistracted time for yourself is one of life's biggest challenges. Finding time to think, to plan, to appreciate, or even time to consider how to be the best mother I can be is one of my ongoing personal challenges.

I hope I'm not alone in routinely questioning my own performance as a mother. And for sure, the days when I've completely lost my patience, raising my voice and shouting an expletive, weren't exactly my most shining moments as a mom. I guess it's human nature to doubt oneself first, and to praise and reward oneself only sporadically.

By my own admission I've become a little overweight. In one of my daughters' words: "Mommy, you are growing." Aah, the indisputable observations of our children.

So, what's more important now? Shall I continue to second-tier my own needs, relegating exercise to "next week" again and again? Or is it time to put my own welfare at the top of the list?

The other day, I sat down to make a list of my top ten favorite activities. To my dismay, I struggled. It had been a long time since I had factored in and made time for my own first choice of activity, much less to actually do any one of the activities on my own "favorites" list.

I've become an expert (and nearly perfect) at organizing my children's lives, buying appropriate food, school supplies, clothing, and shoes. I take time to research our family's decisions regarding childcare, education and the never-ending requests our children make.

I've certainly heard the sound advice before. Make time for yourself. Set boundaries. At times I feel my inner voice talking to me, inviting me to go for it. "Take five," it says.

And it goes on, admonishing me to work myself in to the hours of my own rigorous schedule. Now, if I can only heed my own advice. At the moment, it's 11:04 p.m., and this time for writing passes as "me time." Hey, I gotta take it when I can.

Here's my thought process. You can try it with me if you like. Let's consider, for our own well-being, as well as for the sake of setting a positive example for our kids, putting the "me" back in Mommy. Let's revisit who we are—that person underneath the mommy, wife and sometimes business person. What do you like? Is it music? Dance? Settling in with a good book?

Let's make a pact to schedule in time for ourselves. We schedule our child's doctor's appointment, or our own dental appointment, without hesitating for even a moment. Those are not negotiable, right? I'm vowing now to set the balance between "three and me," so that "me" gets its fair share of love and attention.

And in case I need additional motivation to offset my guilt reflex that automatically kicks in, I'm going to remind myself, it's for the sake of my children, too.

Choices

I get a lot of reactions from passersby. The question that I hear, nearly every time I'm out with the girls is "Are they triplets?"

"Yes, they are." I respond with a smile, because contemplating the fact that I have the huge and lucky fortune of having three pretty little daughters, all at once, always makes me smile. Sometimes the mouth of the person who asked the question drops open, and no words come out.

"You lucky!" my Vietnamese manicurist recently exclaimed.

Others bow at me in appreciation, apparently recognizing the enormity of my parenting task.

I imagine that raising three girls of the same age may be akin to having three girls of different ages, but of course I'm guessing. My three daughters just happen to be the same age, with the same birthday, and in the same class at school. But that's where the similarity ends.

We've been told that it's recommended to separate twins or triplets, and to enroll multiples in different classes to promote their individuality and avoid their tendency to either take comfort in or rely upon their siblings. If we'd had that choice in the French language immersion school we selected, we most likely would have separated the girls that way.

As it is, the girls don't learn at the same pace, even with the same circumstances and teachers. Lily finishes her homework in one day without being told, and asks for more. Everest is happy to do her homework when asked, with a smile and without too much apparent difficulty. Mia, challenged by school, is not particularly interested in the task of demonstrating what she's learned each day. Assuming that she has learned something, that is. We haven't yet determined how to best teach our "eldest." Thankfully, she hasn't lost her motivation. She recently asked me how to spell over a dozen words while working studiously with pencil and paper, and she subsequently presented me what could best be described as a rhyming rap (at least it would be that if we set it to music).

I hope that our choices as parents don't impose too many future limitations on our girls.

Lily asked me the other day, "Why are we learning French?"

I found myself stumbling through my answer because all of our reasons at the time of enrollment have become a dull memory. I couldn't exactly say "uh, it seemed like a really good idea at the time?" My mind drew a blank in the face of her question. It was a choice, and that was all.

I do recall thinking that the French pre-kinder education was a good educational value, at only $2,000 more per year per child than the English-only program. And I'm sure our thinking extended to the fact that we could take family trips to France. That would certainly be one way we'd be happy to support our children's education.

Somehow it came up a day or two after Lily's question on the matter, that what concerned her specifically was, I am paraphrasing now, "When in the hell am I going to learn to read and write English?"

"Good question," I thought to myself. The public magnet

immersion school, in its infinite wisdom, delayed teaching English reading and writing until the third grade to allow the children the opportunity to master the foreign language before embarking upon the task of teaching good old-fashioned English. Who were we to argue?

And the tuition was free, a savings of roughly $50,000 per year from the private school the girls went to for Pre-kindergarten and Kindergarten. Let me see...$50,000, for English and French at the same time...or zero, plus voluntary donations, for the magnet school with a slight delay in English learning? Although we suspected that the private school education might be better than that which the public school offered, we made the switch. The savings was too big to turn down. Turns out, our desire for the best education possible for our children did come at a price, and it was a price we weren't willing to pay. My husband joked that in four years we'd be able to buy some real estate in the desert with the savings. Are our priorities all f'd up?

We've engaged a private home tutor for our daughter with the less than an avid interest in learning. I recognize my own limitations as a parent—shortness of temper and impatience being high on the list. So giving someone else the task of ensuring that my daughter is keeping up with the elementary school curriculum seems to be a good solution. Maybe with that concern freed up, I can devote a few more moments to helping my other two girls excel to the best of their respective abilities as well. And perhaps I'll even take some time along the way for myself.

Parting Thoughts

Patience. It takes a lot. Humility. Perhaps even more.

As a parent, I've needed to be willing to take objective stock of my weaknesses while remembering to applaud my strengths. I've noticed the relevance of making note of the things that bring me pleasure and the importance of scheduling time to do those things as often as possible.

I try to look for and see the joy in each day, including unexpected nice surprises (today my husband picked up the girls from school, giving me time to write these thoughts down on paper). I've made it a practice to find the fun in every day experiences, including an ordinary family dinner together. I like making note of these happy moments…just thinking about what I love and appreciate gives me a lift, especially when life feels overwhelming. And it's certainly better than focusing on the opposite.

Thanks for letting me share my journey with you.

And thank you for being my friend and listener, in your reading of my life experiences. I wish you love, joy, adventure, and more love, on your own life path.

May the universe bring you and yours many blessings!

Answers to Commonly Asked Questions

A few questions posed by my some of my earliest readers (but after our final round of edits) are addressed here for your further reading pleasure.

Reader: *What happened to your interest in music? Did you ever pursue it?*

Carol: Music has stayed in my life, albeit at a lower priority, first to earning a living, then to raising my girls. During my early career days I did some semi-professional performing as a singer. These days I just berate myself for having too little patience to teach my kids the piano.

Reader: *Do you speak French?*

Carol: Yes. My earliest motivation for learning French was that I wanted to be able to understand the occasional French phrase I would come across in my recreational fiction reading. I spent my junior year of college in France and became almost, not quite, fluent. My language skills help me to support our girls in their French language education.

Reader: *Did you enjoy economics at all?*
Carol: Eh.

Reader: *Did your experience in acquiescing to your father's preferences about college affect your intentions regarding your daughters feeling free to pursue their own interests?*

Carol: The short answer is "yes," I do hope that the girls each find their passion and are able to pursue it as their livelihood. But I don't know that I'd characterize my experience with my dad as acquiescence. I know that he did what he felt was right as a parent. As a result I was faced with the choice of college being paid for, versus me paying for it myself. The latter felt like too much for me to take on. In hindsight, at the age of sixteen, I was too young to be making such an important life decision. That event in my life definitely factored into our decision to have the girls repeat kindergarten, so that they would be older and hopefully more mature when making life altering decisions such as choices relating to college and field of study.

Reader: *Have any of the girls maintained an interest in acting?*

Carol: At the moment none of them appear to have any interest in acting. Perhaps that's for the best…

Reader: *What was the nature of your 40 questions to Simon?*

Carol: My questions mostly revolved around the subject of marriage and family. I wanted to be sure Simon had the same long-term vision for his life as I did for mine.

Reader: *What time do you wake up?*

Carol: Normally, 7 a.m.—except when I find myself wide awake in the middle of the night and I decide to get up for a snack and to write for several hours to tire myself out to the point of exhaustion so that I can sleep. Then I might not wake up until 9:30 or even 10:00 a.m., circumstances permitting, such as Simon being available for any parental vigilance required.

Reader: *Were you able to work at all during the latter stages of your pregnancy?*

Carol: Yes. I did my best, anyway. I propped my laptop on the bed or sofa while lying on my side. It wasn't very comfortable. A few weeks later we purchased a small desk on wheels that slid under the bed, and that was much better.

Reader: *Were your mom and dad present at the birth? Are they active grandparents? Do you have help from siblings?*

Carol: I honestly don't remember. I don't think so, but I could be wrong. C-sections are messy procedures, and only my husband was in the delivery room (along with the twenty or so medical professionals that made up the delivery team of my doctor and his assistants). Mom and Dad are in their senior years, but they do still occasionally babysit. They are an integral part of our family circle. None of the girls' aunts and uncles live especially close. They support us with visits, cards and presents for the girls. It's been years since any of them have offered to babysit. Maybe I wasn't appreciative enough when they did.

Reader: *Has your relationship with your husband changed since the triplets were born?*

Carol: Yes! It's interesting how the responsibility we each feel to take care of our daughters has unintentionally impacted how we interact with each other. Division of labor is a tricky subject that comes up again and again. Thankfully we love each other, and this is the underlying element that helps dilute the stresses that arise, as they often do. We make it a priority to go out to dinner or the movies, just the two of us, or out to an occasional concert. This time alone together helps us to nurture our relationship and to give us time to be just "us."

Resources

The following multiple birth, parenting, and child care resources may be helpful to you and your family. Any reference to a specific product, organization, or service does not constitute or imply an endorsement by the author.

- 15 Minute Miracle www.15minutemiracle.com
- Care.com, an online service matching care providers with employers.
- Center for the Study of Multiple Birth, www.multiplebirth.com
- Child Entertainment Laws, Wage and Hour Division, U.S. Department of Labor, www.dol.gov/whd/state/childentertain.htm
- Hicks, Ester and Jerry, *Ask and it is Given: Learning to Manifest Your Desires* (Hay House, 2004).

- Honda Motor Co., www.honda.com
- Kids Klub, a Pasadena, California-based day care center, www.kidsklubcdc.com
- Klauser, Henriette Anne, *Write It Down, Make It Happen: Knowing What You Want And Getting It* (Fireside Books, 2001).
- Landmark Worldwide, a company that offers personal and professional growth, training and development services, www.landmarkworldwide.com
- Mini-crib, Million Dollar Baby, www.milliondollarbaby.com
- Multiples of America, www.multiplesofamerica.org
- National Center for Health Statistics, Centers for Disease Control and Prevention, "Multiple Births." www.cdc.gov/nchs/fastats/multiple.htm
- Paloma Jackson, Paloma Model and Talent (children's talent agent), www.palomamodelandtalent.com
- Raising Multiples, www.raisingmultiples.org
- West Los Angeles Parents of Multiples (WLAPOM), www.wlapom.org

Acknowledgements

In this busy and hectic world, with electronics dominating our lives and person to person contact becoming nearly extinct, I have found my own personal balance in life. That doesn't mean not busy, and it doesn't mean no pressures or challenges. It just means that as the hours go by in the course of my days, I have been able to keep in perspective what is most important for me, which is the love I cherish between me and those in my family.

I'd like to take a moment to thank the people in my life who love and support me, and especially those who make me laugh or who bring a smile to my face. In no particular order, this includes, my husband and three children, who love me and give me frequent supporting hugs, and who provided the inspiration for this book.

I'd like to thank my parents, who at 88 and 91 still

routinely sing my praises, and my sister, who has always applauded my creative efforts in life.

I'd like to acknowledge Ellen Snortland, my own personal Gloria Allred, a champion of women and who provided the context in which the majority of these musings were first aired and vetted, and who has continued to be a cheerleader supporting my writing and providing useful feedback. I'd like to also thank the women in Ellen's writer's workshop, many of whom took the time to read my earlier drafts and to provide input and critical helpful feedback.

I'd like to thank Laurel Airica, who helped facilitate two full rounds of edits, Sharon Goldinger from Pplspeak, who provided encouragement and guidance during the editing process, and Anton Mack, Christine D'Angelo, Baz Here, and Bambi Here, who performed the manuscript's final edits. I'd like to thank Milton Simpson, who has been a nearly lifelong friend, and who helped me navigate the final steps in getting this book out into the universe, and Gary Crossey of IRISHGUY Design Studio, who with his artistry created the perfect book cover.

I'd like to thank Evelyne Claude Blumberg, who through her coaching has helped me to stay grounded in life. I am also grateful for the support of our girls' teachers, tutors, and babysitters, all of whom lightened my load and my stress levels, freeing me to be the most loving mom that I can be.

Last but not least, I'd like to thank Dr. Bryan S. Jick and the medical staff at Huntington Hospital in Pasadena, California, who safely brought our daughters into this world, and Dr. Michele L. Evans and Dr. Hemant B. Upadhyaya, who helped in the earliest stages of our daughters' infant lives. I am eternally grateful for their care and support.

BALANCING THREE

For information about ordering additional copies
or copyright permissions, please contact ACME Publishing:
(626) 227-1188 extension 108.

For press and speaking engagements, please contact
Carol Lefkowitz Jones
(626) 227-1188 extension 101.

www.balancingthree.com